A Zen Life of Bodhisattvas

Rafe Martin

A Zen Life of Bodhisattvas
Rafe Martin

Published by
The Sumeru Press Inc.
PO Box 75, Manotick Main Post Office,
Manotick, ON, Canada K4M 1A2

Copyright © 2023 by Rafe Martin
Cover painting: "Two Trees" by Rafe Martin
Interior photos of Bodhisattvas at Endless Path Zendo by Rafe Martin

ISBN 978-1-896559-99-5

All rights reserved. No part of this book may be reproduced, stored in a retrieval system, or transcribed in any form or by any means—electronic, mechanical, photocopying, recording, or otherwise—without the prior written permission of the publisher.

LIBRARY AND ARCHIVES CANADA CATALOGUING IN PUBLICATION

Title: A Zen life of bodhisattvas / Rafe Martin.
Names: Martin, Rafe, 1946- author.
Description: Includes bibliographical references.
Identifiers: Canadiana 20230549047 | ISBN 9781896559995 (softcover)
Subjects: LCSH: Bodhisattva (The concept) | LCSH: Bodhisattvas. | LCSH: Zen Buddhism.
Classification: LCC BQ4293 .M37 2023 | DDC 294.3/61—dc23

 For more information about The Sumeru Press visit us at sumeru-books.com

Though we find clear waters reaching to the vast blue sky
    in autumn:
How can it compare with a hazy moon on a spring night!
Most people want it pure white,
But sweep as you will, you can never empty the mind.
    Keizan Jokin, *Transmission of the Light (Denkoroku)*

    The two plum-trees:
    I love their blooming,
    One early, one later.
        Buson

Contents

Foreword and Thanks 7
Introduction 9

Section I: Bodhisattvas

1 The Way of Growing-up Beings 13
2 Manjusri, Bodhisattva of Wisdom:
   Patron of the Zen Sitting Hall. 29
3 Meeting Manjusri, Bodhisattva of Wisdom, Face-to-Face 41
4 Manjusri Fails: A Woman Comes Out of Meditation. 53
5 The Bodhisattva of Great Compassion:
   Kannon, Kanjizai, Kwan-Yin, Avalokitesvara 65
6 Hands and Eyes of the Bodhisattva of Great Compassion. . . . 77
7 Maitreya Bodhisattva and the Dream Within a Dream:
   Yang-shan's Sermon from the Third Seat. 85
8 The Bodhisattva Samantabhadra: A Buddhist Folktale 105

Section 2: THE Bodhisattva

Introduction: The Buddha as *The* Bodhisattva 111
9 Why Be Born Human? The Bodhisattva Makes a Mistake . . . 115
10 Bodhisattvas We Live Among: Plants, Trees, and Aspiration . 131
11 The Bodhisattva Saves the Realm—as the Consciousness
   of a Tree 139

Section 3: The Way of the Ordinary Bodhisattva

12 A Pillar of Zen: Memorial for Roshi Philip Kapleau. 159
13 On Zen and Failure. 169
14 Painting of A Rice Cake: Creative Imagination and the
    Way of the Bodhisattva. 179

Appendices

Zen Chants. 187
Bibliography 193

Foreword and Thanks

Bodhisattvas showed up to help bring this book to life. These were, first of all, my critical readers—Deborah Dallinger, Larry McSpadden, David Harrison, Donna Thomson, Greg Sheldon, and Rose Martin. The points they each raised—and the errors they caught—helped this book mature and become better, much better, than it would have otherwise been. Rose Martin, who not only lived from the start with the evolving manuscript but with its author—no easy task!—gave an especially careful reading to the manuscript that, combined with her long experience of Zen practice and Buddhist tradition, raised vital points for clarification and attention.

Thanks are especially due to the Sangha of Endless Path Zendo for allowing me to try out each of the book's chapters as teishos (Dharma talks) on them—sometimes more than once! Hearing aloud what I'd put down on the page helped me immensely in clarifying each chapter, getting a sense of whether the sequence of chapters worked, all while (hopefully) sticking to the point.

I'm also grateful to the particular encouragement I received from Zen teachers Sunyana Graef, Roshi, of the Vermont Zen Center and Casa Zen, Costa Rica; Taigen Henderson, Roshi, of the Toronto Zen Centre, and Hoag Holmgren of Rollinsville Zen Center. Years ago, when I was in a workshop with poet Robert Bly, he offered these encouraging words: "Having companions increases our courage." How true!

Finally, thanks, to John Negru (Karma Yönten Gyatso), dedicated Buddhist publisher of Sumeru Books. He made this book the reality you now hold in your hands.

Many hands, eyes, and ears made the work light. Bows to all!

Rafe Jnan Martin
Endless Path Zendo
2023

Introduction

How old is the Bodhisattva Manjusri this year?
Introductory koan

This book is a continuation or companion to my book, *A Zen Life of Buddha* (Sumeru, 2022), which explored the centrality of the Buddha's historic and legendary life to ongoing Zen practice. It also looked at the ancient Vow of the Bodhisattva as being what Zen practice is really all about.

In this book we'll look at the nature of that Vow, and the nature and role of bodhisattvas themselves, the greatly wise and compassionate beings at the intimate core of daily Zen practice.

The book's organization is simple. It is arranged in three sections as follows:

The first section, titled "Bodhisattvas," explores who or what bodhisattvas are, how they're seen in Zen tradition, and whether they are even real or not. The focus is on the two bodhisattvas most central to Zen: Manjusri, Bodhisattva of Wisdom, and Avalokitesvara, Bodhisattva of Compassion, two archetypal ways of understanding our own Mind. We'll look too at the bodhisattvas Maitreya and Samantabhadra, who also appear in Zen tradition. Koans will serve as our gateless gateway into this exploration, along with a bit of Buddhist folklore as well.

The second section, "The Bodhisattva," looks at the Buddha even before he was the Buddha, i.e., the actual historic figure, Buddha Shakyamuni, 2500 years ago. Jataka tales, traditional past life tales of the Buddha as he matured along the Way of the Bodhisattva toward Buddhahood, will be our focus. Commentary on each tale from a Zen perspective will connect ancient myth and folklore to the realities of daily Zen practice.

The third and final section, "Ordinary Bodhisattvas," moves from the ideal to the real, and to the life of an ordinary person doing their best to actualize the Way of the Bodhisattva today. It will also explore failure, the painful inevitability of coming up short that underlies the Way of the Bodhisattva. For it is only by the challenges we face in trying, failing, getting back up and trying again that we proceed along the Bodhisattva Way. (The Sunday painter who aims to one day become a Rembrandt of Picasso, must expect that each painting will not yet be quite "it.") We'll look briefly, too, at the connection of creative imagination to Bodhisattva Vows.

To be clear, this is not going to be a scholarly or exhaustive study. Rather, it's a personal expression of my own more than 50 years of formal Zen practice and more than ten years of Zen teaching, first as an apprentice and then as a fully Dharma transmitted Zen teacher. I take my lead from my betters, in this case, the Japanese Zen monk-poet, Ryokan (1751–1838):

> The wind brings
> enough fallen leaves
> to make a fire

# Section I

Bodhisattvas

1

The Way of Growing-up Beings

... Zen is one of the most accessible paths to growing up as a human being. And by 'growing up,' I simply mean becoming aware of our habitual unconscious self-centeredness, and not continuing to build a comfy nest there, not continuing to cling to that, not keeping it in the driver's seat but gradually – and suddenly – to see through it and let it go, so that more and more of whatever we already, selflessly, actually are, can function in and as this life.

Rafe Martin, interviewed by Rick McDaniel,
Further Zen Conversations

As a vital branch of Mahayana (Great Way) Buddhism, Zen Buddhism holds that great bodhisattvas, spiritually advanced "wisdom beings" ("bodhi" in Sanskrit is wisdom and "sattva," being), whose sole purpose is saving all living things from suffering, exist all around us. Having freed themselves from habitual self-centeredness, they are at compassionate play throughout the many worlds.

Zen holds that, along with such deeply realized bodhisattvas, there are countless other less advanced ones, many of whom may be unknown even to themselves. But when things get dark, they begin to shine out like stars in the vastness of night. These are the ordinary, good-hearted people who turn up when the going gets rough, people you can count on to do the right thing. Their humanity, courage, and kindness—traits not owned by any one religion, race, gender, or, perhaps, even species—marks their presence. Whether or not they uphold formal spiritual belief or practice is beside the point. They embody and enact the ancient

Way, making truly *human* life possible for us all.

And then there's us, you and me, who Zen also kindly calls "bodhisattvas," now working at maturing as we persevere through life's ups and downs.

In Buddhist countries entire movements have been inspired by the bodhisattva ideal.

In the Anguttana Nikaya, the Buddha says that those who build causeways and bridges will make much merit for themselves. King Asoka took this as a cue to have roads straightened and repaired, to have them lined with trees and to have wells dug at regular intervals along them.

Numerous records from the Buddhist period in India mention similar good works. A 15th century Tibetan saint built an iron chain suspension bridge that was still in use in the 1950's. In medieval Japan building roads and bridges as an act of piety became almost an obsession. Monks and nuns were forever touring the country collecting funds for such projects and usually the whole community participated in the actual construction. A document dated 1276 concerning the construction of a bridge over the Midori River says: "People of high and low estate crowd on either bank, bickering constantly. People and horses vied to board small boats that then capsize, drowning their passengers". The monk who built his bridge says he did so because : "When we see a dangerous situation, we must make it safe, for the Buddha has compassion for people". Before the rise of the modern states with public works departments, the Buddhist enthusiasm for building roads and bridges had a significant role to play in developing trade, communications, the spread of ideas and generally lessening of the hardships of life.[1]

Zen Master Hakuin, (1686–1769) perhaps the most significant Japanese Zen teacher in the last 300 years, helped build a bridge at a dangerous river crossing. His motivation was as follows:

> When I visited Jissō-ji in Tōrin three or four days later, we had to cross the river again. The porters said, "It's a dangerous crossing. The river often overflows two or three times in a single month. People are carried away and sometimes drown." Again I thought, "Putting up a bridge here is of vital importance, and would be a deed of the greatest virtue as well. If lay people and priests from this area were to combine their efforts, such a project should not be too difficult to accomplish. Done little by little, in small steps, it should not take too long to complete. An undertaking such as this, which would provide great relief to people, can also be seen as a kind of skillful means, promoting the salvation of sentient beings."
>
> With that in mind, I made up a small booklet to serve as a roster in which to list the names of people who contribute donations to the project. As a start, I donated the four strings of coins I had received for the lectures. I also composed a verse, which I inscribed on the roster as a preface. I made copies to give to the priests of four of Ryōtan-ji's subtemples: Daitsū-an, Jikō-an, Genkai-an, and Entsū-an. A small start, the first step in a journey of a thousand leagues, but my hope is that the project will eventually grow and assume mountainous proportions.

---

1   https://www.buddhanet.net/e-learning/dharmadata/fdd54.htm

The verse:

> Erecting a bamboo
> bridge to span a raging
> mountain torrent
> Far excels the merit
> of building pagodas
> throughout the land.
> Hearing of the flooding
> during the spring and
> autumn rains,
> How could anyone sit
> by knowing people will come to harm?
>
> "Preface for a Roster Listing Donors for the Construction of a New Bridge at Yatsuyahata", *Complete Poison Blossoms from a Thicket of Thorn: The Zen Records of Hakuin Zenji*, trans. Norman Waddell

Such compassionate activity goes back to an ideal set in place by the Buddha himself, 2,500 years ago. In the Kulavaka Jataka, one of his past-life tales, he tells of a time when he was a bodhisattva in a distant past life, who dedicated himself to removing boulders from roads, cutting down trees that might break wagon wheels and axles, and building bridges, water tanks, and rest houses to benefit the lives of others.

Buddhist tradition asserts that our actual nature, yours, mine, and everyone's, is already, from the start, that of a buddha or bodhisattva. That each of us, immature and limited as we are, is a wise and compassionate being. Or could be, if we only knew it. Our problem is that we don't know it, that we've forgotten our original nature, and because of this fundamental ignorance, we can—and do—not just fail to act compassionately, but go sadly off-track, often to catastrophic effect. Hence our world today, with its problems of classism, nationalism, racism, misogyny, environmental destruction, and more.

We can choose to correct our fundamental error (and eventually, the ills that spring from it) through what we rather tamely call "spiritual practice." We can begin to set things right by awakening to our actual nature and, then, learning to live from it, in light of it. This is the essence of Zen practice. We practice Zen to awake to Original Nature, and then actualize it in our lives, maturing as beginner bodhisattvas. Nyogen Senzaki, a venerable 20th century Japanese Zen teacher, used to address his students as "Dear Bodhisattvas." Koan 74 in *The Blue Cliff Record* titled "Chin Niu's Rice Pail," includes:

> Every day at mealtime, master Chin Niu would himself bring the pail of boiled rice and do a dance in front of the monk's hall. Laughing loudly, he would say, "Dear bodhisattvas, come and eat."

So Senzaki Sensei was speaking from the heart of the tradition.

Buddhas, (who've gone beyond even being bodhisattvas), are so fully realized and awakened they don't need to *think* of wisdom and compassion at all, anymore. As their entire nature *is* wisdom and compassion, no self-centered thoughts of trying to help or of becoming wise remain. Fully grounded in Reality, they simply help and *are* wise. It is their nature to do and be so. And, so, they outshine bodhisattvas—those who are still hard at work saving, and helping, and choosing not to enter nirvana in order to continue helping, endlessly. This attachment to saving others is said to be the last trace of a bodhisattva's ancient habit of self-centeredness, now refined to the utmost degree.

Zen master Hakuin said, "Zen Buddhism is like an ocean: the farther you go into it, the deeper it gets. It's like a mountain, the more you climb it, the higher it gets." Simply put, the Way of the Bodhisattva is the way of ongoing practice-realization. And what is the wisdom of such "wisdom beings"? I'd say it's a matter of wisely choosing to mature, to grow-up beyond our habitual, unconscious, self-centeredness. Which means, they are not simply nice people or do-gooders. Basically, in Zen, a bodhisattva is you or me, if we choose to do the work of freeing ourselves from the habitual compulsions of a self-centered life.

In Zen, we do this work of maturing by practicing, which means sitting in zazen, focusing on counting the breath: this one, this two, and so on, up to ten and starting at one again, or by fully experiencing this breath, or by working with a teacher and learning to absorb ourselves in a koan so fully that there's no room left for our old, habitual, "me, myself, and I" kind of thinking to claim center stage. Instead, there is just this breath, this koan point, this *vroom* of a car passing in the street, this *Caw!* of the crow, this ache in the knee, this un-self-centered intimacy with what IS. This is our start, our entrance into living a richer, wiser life, a life that begins with being less caught up in ideas of ourselves and, so, less likely to ignore what's right in front of us: this tree, this star, this breath, this person. The compassion of the Way of the Bodhisattva starts here. From this foundation of formal practice, we work at embodying its selfless insight into how we live, how we actually interact with everyone and everything around us. So Zen practice really involves a long process of maturing.

Buddhist tradition says that there are spiritually maturing beings who have been at it so long, that they're now *great* wisdom beings, or mahasattvas ("maha" is "great," "sattva" is "being"). It's said that these greatly advanced bodhisattvas can take any form to aid suffering beings, and can even be petitioned for aid. Many Zen Buddhist centers and temples have areas set aside where practitioners can sit before figures of such advanced bodhisattvas. When we feel lost or stuck or overwhelmed, their presence can remind us of our own potential for

The Way of Growing-up Beings

wisdom and compassion. Sitting before them can be deeply encouraging. But the advanced bodhisattva-mahasattvas embodied in sculpture and paintings are not gods. They were ordinary people who chose to work on themselves, who realized enlightenment, or intimacy, and came forward from there, confirmed in a selfless commitment to be of benefit to all.

The two greatest bodhisattvas at the core of Zen Buddhism are Manjusri, Bodhisattva of Wisdom, (in Japan he may be known as Monju, in China as Wenshu), and Avalokitesvara, Bodhisattva of Compassion, (Kannon, Kanjizai, or Kwannon in Japan, Kwan-yin in China). The bodhisattvas Manjusri and Kannon show the natural pairing of wisdom and compassion that is the heart of Zen practice and teaching.

Samantabhadra, (Fugen in Japan) Bodhisattva of Compassionate *Action*, while less well-known in the West, remains a mainstay of Asian Zen, where he appears on Zen Buddhist altars, seated on the Buddha's right, paired with Manjusri on the Buddha's left. Iconographically, Samantabhadra is seated on an elephant, and Manjusri on a lion. There is also Maitreya Bodhisattva (Miroku in Japan), who is said to now be in the Tushita Heavens, getting ready to liberate all beings once he's back on Earth as our next full Buddha.

While a focus on these particular bodhisattvas may seem arbitrary, especially given that other Buddhist traditions, such as Vajrayana, recognize *many* bodhisattvas, these few remain the important ones for Zen. Yasutani Roshi, the 20th century Japanese teacher so central to the transmission of koan training to the West, wrote:

> Most Buddhist scholars say that Kwannon is our compassionate mind but that there is no concrete Bodhisattva existing outside us. This statement is only half true. It is a theoretical interpretation of Kwannon and omits the actual interpretation. For every theory

there is an underlying fact. Theory and fact must exist simultaneously; if not, either the theory is false or the fact is misunderstood.

Kwannon Bodhisattva is indeed our compassionate mind, and if we cultivate this compassion we can all become Kwannon Bodhisattva. In this sense there are many Kwannons in the world. Kwannon literally means '"to hear others' anxieties intuitively". A person who saves others and who is full of compassion by virtue of this intuitive faculty is called Kwannon Bodhisattva.

Without exception we all have the sympathetic spirit of Kwannon.

Because of our misconception about the ego, however, we have lost this intuitive feeling ...

Buddhism encourages us to realize the fact that the concept of ego is an illusion. Then it helps us to awaken our inherent sympathetic spirit. As a means to this end Buddhism teaches us to do charitable work. This is the theoretical interpretation of Kwannon Bodhisattva.

As long as we have Kwannon's virtue we cannot deny that the real Kwannon who cultivates this virtue and uses his compassion one hundred per cent really does exist ...

To further clarify this actual interpretation let me explain Moniu Bodhisattva and Fugen Bodhisattva. According to the theoretical interpretation Monju is our enlightened wisdom and Fugen is our complete compassionate mind which evolves from this enlightened wisdom. This interpretation is correct. However to say that no real Bodhisattvas like Monju or Fugen exist is an error... Both Bodhisattvas appear in Buddhist sutras and scriptures quite frequently. It is the natural and correct attitude of a Buddhist to believe in the actual existence of these two Bodhisattvas.

There is one more important Bodhisattva whom we must not forget. His name is Maitreya Bodhisattva (Miroku). He was assigned to be the successor of Shakyamuni Buddha and will appear in this world 5,670,000,000 years after Buddha's death. It is said that he is now in Tosotsu Heaven preaching to heavenly beings and that when Buddhism disappears from this world he will become Buddha.

Yasutani Roshi, *Eight Beliefs in Buddhism*

Such *great* bodhisattvas are the Rembrandts, Van Goghs and Picassos of Zen. Compared to them we are the Sunday painters, the hobbyists still learning to set up our easels, choose our brushes, and get something down on canvas. Still, if even hobbyists persist, who knows what they might become capable of creating?

In short, Zen is a practical, accessible way of walking the Path of the Bodhisattva and of actualizing the Great Vow, which can be summed up as: "Whatever be the highest perfection of the human mind, may I realize it for the benefit of all that lives!" (Lama Govinda, *Foundations of Tibetan Mysticism*.) Zen Master Hakuin wrote:

> In Chinese, he's "the sentient being of great heart."
> Entering the three ways, [the three ways are the realms
>   of hungry ghosts, animals, and hell dwellers] he
>   takes on our suffering.
> Joyfully appearing unbidden throughout the world.
> Vowing not to accept the fruit of partial awakening,
> He deepens his attainment in working to save others.

> Even should the great void completely cease to exist,
> His struggle to save sentient beings would never end.
> *Complete Poison Blossom from a Thicket of Thorn:*
> *The Records of Hakuin Zenji.* Waddell

Classical Buddhism says that the length of any aspiring bodhisattva's spiritual career, starting from their initial vow to their complete realization of Innate Buddhahood, will be $3 \times 10^{15} \times 320 \times 10^6$ years or, four times nine hundred sixty thousand million billion billion billion billion years. In essence, it's going to take an unimaginably long time, a time beyond all conceptual understanding. (Reading between the lines and from a Zen perspective, this also suggests that right now, beyond all concepts including those of time and space, Original Nature is already accessible.)

Master Dogen, in a section of the *Shobogenzo* (*Eye of the Treasury of the True Dharma*) titled "Painting of a Rice Cake," wrote, that to paint a picture of Buddha (i.e., to become one), we use not paints and brushes, but "countless kalpas of assiduous practice." As to what the length of a kalpa might be, classical Buddhism says that a kalpa is the time it would take a deva, or god of a higher realm, who swoops down to Earth once every hundred years and brushes the top of a great mountain with the sleeve of his or her silken robe, to wear that mountain down to the ground. Torei Zenji, Hakuin's heir, emphasized that Zen students, motivated by bodhisattva vows, should understand that their training will necessarily entail a long maturation. In his view, kensho—a first and usually shallow glimpse of self-nature—is simply where we begin. For those who persist, additional kenshos and eventually, deeper and more complete ones, called "satori," will follow. In the meantime, our character is tested, and our emerging skills improve through the challenges of living.

In the Buddha's past life (jataka) tales, stories of his own path as a bodhisattva, an animal or even a tree might be more spiritually evolved than a human being. Is this mere religious fantasy? Well, dogs do run through flames to save people, dolphins have pushed drowning swimmers to shore, whales have protected snorkelers from sharks, orcas have guided boaters to safe harbors, recently a pod of sperm whales adopted a lonely, deformed dolphin, and trees and plants which give us the oxygen we need to breathe, transformed what was once a barren rock of a planet into a garden. What might these *facts* be saying about the nature of our world?

From a Buddhist perspective life is itself bodhisattvic. Essentially. Yet, given the chaotic, even horrific events of history, isn't such a view childishly naive? Do we have to shut our eyes to reality to become Zen Buddhists? The Four Vows, or Great Vows for All, which Zen students recite at the conclusion of periods of formal zazen, seem pretty impossible. At Endless Path Zendo, the version we use (based on a translation by Robert Aitken Roshi) goes like this:

> The many beings are numberless,
> I vow to free them all;
> Greed hatred and ignorance rise endlessly,
> I vow to abandon them all;
> Dharma gates are countless,
> I vow to wake to them all;
> Buddha's Way is unattainable,
> I vow to embody it all.

How could anyone accomplish such things—free or save all beings; become free oneself of all ignorance, greed, and hatred; see life and its difficulties as a source of endless opportunity for greater personal insight and depth; and finally, attain what can't be attained? Master Hakuin's great disciple, Torei Enji, formulated an especially personal and heart-felt Bodhisattva Vow that goes like this:

I am only a simple disciple, but I offer these respectful words.

When I regard the true nature of the many dharmas, I find them all to be sacred forms of the Tathagata's never-failing essence. Each particle of matter, each moment, is no other than the Tathagata's inexpressible radiance.

With this realization, our virtuous ancestors gave tender care to beasts and birds with compassionate minds and hearts. Among us, in our own daily lives, who is not reverently grateful for the protections of life: food, drink, and clothing! Though they are inanimate things, they are nonetheless the warm flesh and blood, the merciful incarnations of Buddha.

All the more, we can be especially sympathetic and affectionate with foolish people, particularly with someone who becomes a sworn enemy and persecutes us with abusive language. That very abuse conveys the Buddha's boundless loving-kindness. It is a compassionate device to liberate us entirely from the mean-spirited delusions we have built up with our wrongful conduct from the beginningless past.

With our open response to such abuse we completely relinquish ourselves, and the most profound and pure faith arises. At the peak of each thought a lotus flower opens, and on each flower there is revealed a Buddha. Everywhere is the Pure Land in its beauty. We see fully the Tathagata's radiant light right where we are.

May we retain this mind and extend it throughout the world so that we and all beings become mature in Buddha's wisdom.

Buddhist tradition says that advanced bodhisattva-mahasattvas who live such vows can appear in any form to help. It is their art form, their play. Ennin, a Japanese Buddhist monk traveling in T'ang era China, reported that when he went to Mt. Wutai, the mountain sacred to Manjusri, Bodhisattva of Wisdom, he found that everyone—monks, nuns, lay men and women—treated even the lowliest person or animal there with exceptional kindness. They'd see a donkey and whisper, "It could be Manjusri! He might have taken this form!" and would treat that animal with the utmost respect, just in case.

Such advanced bodhisattvas, we're told, might even surprise us with actions that look like anything *but* help. So the storm that grounds our plane and ruins our plans might be a bodhisattva doing his or her thing, creating a delay to save us from ... who knows what? Or a bodhisattva could be the one dialing that ringing phone which, when we pick it up, has no one on the line. Here's a true story ... A young woman with a child on her hip was making dinner when the phone rang out in the living room. She stepped from the kitchen to answer, but there was no one on the line. She'd just started back for the kitchen, when BOOM! the pressure cooker she was using to make spaghetti sauce blew, hurling its heavy lid to the ceiling and spraying the whole kitchen with boiling sauce. The lid hadn't been locked down right. If it hadn't been for that phone call, she and the child would have been standing right next to the stove, where they could have been blinded, maimed, or even killed. Had they been saved from injury or death by the Wrong-Number-Bodhisattva who dialed them up just in time?

Maybe. Perhaps. Even so, can we depend on miraculous salvations? Should they be articles of Zen Buddhist faith? Wouldn't it be foolish to go around proclaiming, "That rude person who cut me off on the highway, forcing me to miss my exit, was a bodhisattva!" Or "That bee sting that put me in the hospital was a bodhisattva." Though faith in the existence of bodhisattvas—beings more spiritually mature than ourselves—makes sense, (especially given what we know about ourselves!), Zen tradition still says that to know who or what bodhisattvas are, we need to know who or what we ourselves are. "What is this self? Where is this self? Who sees colors with the eyes, hears sounds with the ears?" To answer such questions, we may point to our heads or hearts and say "within" – but where *is* that? Is the self male or female, old or young, wise or foolish? In time, we all will face unanswerable questions: Who am I? Why was I born? Why must I die? Why am I here? Why, if we live in a beneficent universe, are there holocausts and killing fields, droughts, famines, tsunamis, and earthquakes? Why all this *suffering*? There is nothing naive about this. Zen does not ask us to put on rose-colored glasses.

In fact, rather than searching for bodhisattvas to save us, Zen says we'd do better to plunge into the questions that truly plague us, and there seek—and find—answers—and, so, mature into, and as, bodhisattvas ourselves. This, after all, is what the Buddha left home to do. This is what Zen Buddhist practice can help us do as well—in our own way and to our own degree. Then again, are bodhisattvas really real?

In 1970, after I'd left graduate school, my wife, Rose (who was pregnant with our first child, Jacob, at the time) and I were living in rural Pennsylvania, an hour or so south of Binghamton, NY. One day, we drove into town—Rose had a dentist appointment—and while she was busy, I took off in our old VW bus to handle errands. I chanced on a gas station run by two old gents in overalls who sold used cars. As I gassed up, we talked. I mentioned the upcoming birth. They looked at me. Then they looked at the VW—an old, un-insulated, rattling, bare metal cargo plane of a van.

"You have a child coming?" they mused. (In their voices I heard echoes of the cartoon rooster, Foghorn Leghorn saying, "Son, I say ... son.") "Well, now," they said, "why don't you take a look at this GMC truck? Step right over here." It was blue, solid, gleaming. Everything about it, from the massive emergency brake, to the rows of thickly padded, removable, bench seats proclaimed: "Industrial Strength".

"Take a drive," they said. I got in and drove away. Such a smooth, solid ride! I had visions of driving with ease up the hill to our old farmhouse through deep winter snows—a risky, bouncing, pedal-to-the-metal feat in our bus. I had visions of nomadic family security. "How much?" I asked, heart in my mouth, when I returned, flush with truck-power, with new dreams and hope. They named a ridiculously low sum, plus the wretched old bus. We shook hands all around. It was a bargain. I picked up Rose and spilled the good news.

I drove back the next day, a check for the truck in my shirt pocket. Five blocks from their gas station and car lot, there was a loud *Bang!* from the engine in the rear. The old VW staggered as if shot, then kept on rolling, though now in a halting, shuddering, groaning, wheezing sort of way. We limped up to the pump where I stopped and mercifully killed the engine. Except for the ticking of overheated metal there was an awful silence. I sat on the peeling leather seat waiting for the smoke to clear. From the haze of my mind rose a helpless, anguished refrain: "Up the creek without a paddle. No truck, not even the old van now. Cash low, baby coming."

The two elderly gents stepped forward. "Well," they said, "you brought the bus. Do you have the check?"

"Yes. Yes, I do. You'll still take it?" I asked, incredulous.

"A deal's a deal," they answered.

"You don't want more money?" I asked in a daze.

"Nope," said the bodhisattvas.

I pulled the crumpled check from my pocket, signed it, and handed it over, then drove off in that heavenly blue (blue, the color of Bhaisyaguru Buddha, the Buddha of Healing) GMC truck. Not long after, I drove that reliable truck serenely down twisting mountain roads in a heavy fog in the middle of the night so Jake could be born with one push in the local hospital. Eight weeks later we loaded our possessions into that big blue truck and moved to Rochester where the truck was eventually named "the Rafemobile'" by the Zen Center, which acquired it from us a year later. They got many years of sturdy yeoman's service from it. It ran and ran as if it possessed a good stout heart under its huge blue hood, and not the mere mechanical assemblage of an engine. It ran as if blessed.

    I sometimes wonder what I would have found if I'd returned to that car lot and gas station—an empty field, wind rippling through long grasses, no cars, flags, banners, pumps; no old gents in overalls, all gone, gone entirely gone? Were those two old guys in overalls bodhisattvas? They certainly seemed so at the time. I have no other explanation for such extraordinarily selfless compassion. They remind me now of Hanshan and Shih-de, those two old Zen loonies up on Cold Mountain, who Zen tradition accepts as having been emanations of Manjusri, Bodhisattva of Wisdom, and Samantabhadra, Bodhisattva of Compassionate Action.

    Still, even if it's true that advanced bodhisattvas surround us, and that even blind donkeys might be or can become great bodhisattvas, our job as Zen students is to embody our own bodhisattva vows and, in small ways, make them real. This is the Path of all growing up wisdom beings. It begins with this breath, this count, this koan. And, while such a path is endless, paradoxically, at the same time, right here, in this fleeting moment, is everything we seek.

> A monk asked Ta-lung:
> "The body of form perishes. What is the eternal body?"
> Ta-lung responded:
> "The mountain flowers bloom like brocade;
> the river between the hills runs blue as indigo."
>   Case 82, *Blue Cliff Record* (*Hekigan roku*)

2

Manjusri, Bodhisattva of Wisdom: Patron of the Zen Sitting Hall

I bow deeply before the great teacher Manjusri
Whose pure clear Dharma body is painted here.
If you see him on the surface of the paper,
You're just digging a well to see white clouds;
If you pursue him apart from this painted image,
You're ambling eastward chasing the setting sun.
See it!!
I bow deeply before the great teacher Manjusri.
> Inscribed by Hakuin, age 35, on his first painting of the Bodhisattva Manjusri. [Waddell. *Complete Poison Blossoms From a Thicket of Thorn.*]

Manjusri, Bodhisattva of Wisdom, patron "saint" of zendos, is the most primary Zen bodhisattva. In Japan, the Buddha sits in the Buddha Hall, but Manjusri, Bodhisattva of Wisdom, presides over the zendo, the realm of formal practice, where he's often shown seated on a lion. Holding a scroll or a lotus in one hand and a sword in the other, he may have the shaved head of a monk—showing himself free of all attachments and concerns—or may be a prince with long hair, flowing robes and jewelry, royally engaged with life.

In traditional Japanese zendos, Manjusri's altar is often in the center of the room, out among the sitters, rather than set higher up and back against the far wall. As the practitioners in such zendos sit on a raised platform, their heads are at the same height as Manjusri's. Sitting in such a zendo you have a sense of fundamental equality. He's not up high, looking down at you. Which makes sense. Seeing things in comparison, relative to one another, creates our ordinary world of highs and lows, bigs and littles, and so on. But when, through attention to the practice, that relative world falls away, Equality awakes. Each thing is suddenly, entirely, vividly, mysteriously Itself. This is Manjusri's realm, Manjusri's experience, Manjusri's wisdom. From this perspective, the life of an ant and the life of an Einstein are of equal worth, each Absolutely itself!

To present such profound Equality, which does not deny but affirms the uniqueness of each thing, the Bodhisattva of Wisdom sits *with* us, not above us. When he swings the delusion cutting sword, he is the power of active practice, cutting through dualistic, self-centered thinking, cutting all into One. His sword of insight is said to simultaneously both kill and give life; when dualistic delusions are cut, the greater, non-dual life emerges. When the sword is held upright it is *prajna*—perfect wisdom's "hair-blown" sword, so sharp that no effort is required; delusions that drift against it are instantly cut. On the lotus in his left hand is the book or scroll that is the Heart of Perfect Wisdom or, Prajnaparamita, whose own heart is "Form is only emptiness, emptiness only form." Things fall into place when Manjusri is around. Wisdom is not something far off, not esoteric. Here's a little verse I wrote back in 2009 as part of my lay ordination:

> Buds on the trees!
> Buds on the trees!
> Manjusri's on his lion.
> All's well with the world.

On an altar with the Buddha, Manjusri may be paired with Samantabhadra. Manjusri, on a lion, presents the fearlessness of the Absolute, the courageous realization of Selfless Emptiness. Samantabhadra, on an elephant, presents the unstoppably active compassion arising *from* Emptiness. Together, they form the two "arms" of the Buddha.

In some Buddhist traditions, Manjusri's wisdom is a matter of learning and intelligence. As his practice is said to strengthen memory and make the mind subtle and sharp, he is sometimes also shown with two young attendants who are themselves on a path of learning. His mantra is *oṃ arapacana dhīḥ*.

But in Zen, Manjusri's wisdom is "gone beyond," opening the path of non-dual Insight, a Knowing beyond understanding. Buddhist tradition says that long ago Manjusri realized full Buddhahood, then decided to stick around and become a bodhisattva again to help others also attain the Way. So he is revered as the teacher of the past seven Buddhas here on Earth. Yamada Roshi, Aitken Roshi's teacher, in a series of unpublished talks on the *Blue Cliff Record* (*Hekigan roku*) koan collection writes:

> You might think it strange that a mere Bodhisattva could be the teacher of Buddhas. But Manjusri can be taken as the symbol for the world of emptiness. No one has

attained Buddhahood without experiencing this world of emptiness. Thus, Manjusri is seen as the one who teaches the Buddhas about that world. In actual fact, however, he was a disciple of Shakyamuni. He is ranked as a great Bodhisattva together with Avalokitesvara and Samantabhadra.

Typically, Manjusri is shown as youthful, because wisdom is always fresh and new, sometimes startlingly so. Which makes sense—how old or stale can "Aha!" be? So he is also known as the Ever-Youthful One. Then again, he can also appear as old and venerable, as wisdom takes years to mature.

At Endless Path Zendo, Manjusri appears in variety of forms. A large Japanese scroll reproduction of Manjusri on a blue lion hangs in the dokusan ("going alone") room, where teacher and student meet "knee to knee, eyeball to eyeball." His hair is in five tufts (signifying the 5 wisdoms that appear when the mind is freed of self-centeredness), and he holds not a sword, but a lotus in one hand and the scroll of Prajnaparamita's "Heart of Perfect Wisdom" in the other. In the zendo, a large bronze Manjusri, (a Chinese version of a Nepalese or Tibetan original) wields a delusion-cutting sword in his right hand, a book of the Prajnaparamita rising on a lotus in his left. A small wooden Manjusri on a lion holds an upright, hair-blown prajna sword and a wisdom scroll as he sits before the Buddha on our main altar. A white porcelain Manjusri, accompanied by two young attendants, looks out over the dokusan line, where sitters wait to enter the teacher's room. His hair is long and he holds a kotsu (teacher's stick), or imperial staff, demonstrating that his personal wishes are in selfless accord with the universe. A wisdom scroll rests on a lotus leaf beside him, and though waves surge beneath his feet, he is at ease, one leg half down, one hand resting lightly on his knee, ready to get up and be of help to all.

Mahayana and Vajrayana Buddhism also include four-armed Manjusris with bow and arrow and spear, as well as various female forms. Tibetan Buddhists acknowledge Yamantaka, "Slayer of Death," the dark blue, many armed, fiercely wrathful form of Manjusri. Surrounded by flames and sporting a bull's head, he is a Dharma guardian, enemy of all self-centered evils.

So, Manjusri, then, may be shown with a book, a sword, a lion, a kotsu, an imperial scepter, and a lotus; with bows and arrows and flames all of which can be signifiers of wisdom. What kind of wisdom? If we want to know in more than purely academic terms, that is, if we want to know it personally, Zen says that we must sink into Mu, into this breath, this count, this specific koan point. And if we do, at some point Manjusri's truly living wisdom may become so clear, we can even find ourselves doubled over in laughter. What relief! All our many accumulated worries, that whole self-centered burden of "me, myself, and I"—and all the sorrows and errors that spring from it—can be gone, having at least momentarily fallen completely away.

Touching base with wisdom's fountain of youth, dropping body and mind, "sinking into Mu," becoming intimate with this count, this breath, this *Caw!* of the crow, doesn't mean that we fall into a vat of spiritual pudding in which distinctions vanish and all is "One." Ants and eagles, stars and snails, hangnails and nine-inch nails are not replaced by "emptiness." "All is One" doesn't erase the uniqueness of each thing; rather it empowers it. Each thing is absolutely unique, literally incomparable. The book or scroll that Manjusri carries, the wisdom that the sword cutting through all dualism reveals, is that "form is only emptiness, emptiness only form." It is not a provisional truth. Which simply means that right now, just as the world, and just as we ourselves are at this moment, it is the truth. It is not a truth held off into an imagined future when we are fully enlightened. It is the truth now, whether we see it or not. Still, wise as he is, enlightened as he is, beyond all self-centered delusions and duality as he is, like us Manjusri still needs to read a manual to fix his carburetor or restart his Kindle.

Nevertheless, in this world of the so-called "10,000 things"—our bustling world of cats, clouds, bugs, people, cell phones, mountains, stars, trees, and rivers—Manjusri functions wisely, for when he swings his delusion-cutting sword, MY tree is cut down, and MY child is gone. Instead, there stands my *Tree*, here comes my *Child*, whole and complete as they've ever been.

But if Manjusri is so wise, how is it that in the *Vimalakirti Sutra*, the wealthy old enlightened Buddhist layman Vimalakirti, lying on his sickbed in a bare room, so easily puts the Great Bodhisattva of Wisdom to shame? Or is Manjusri, ever selflessly skillful, acting as a foil so that he and Vimalakirti working together, can put on a splendid Dharma show? Here's *Blue Cliff Record* case 84, "Vimalakirti's Gate of Non-Duality"—

> Vimalakirti asked Manjusri, "What is the Bodhisattva's Dharma gate of non-duality?"
>
> Manjusri answered, "To my mind, in all dharmas there are no words, no preaching, no demonstration, and no recognition. It is beyond all questions and answers. That is entering the Dharma gate of non-duality."
>
> Then Manjusri asked Vimalakirti, "Each of us has had his say. Now tell us, good man, what is the bodhisattva's entry into the Dharma gate of non-duality?"
>
> [Hsueh Tou (Setcho) commented, saying, "What did Vimalakirti say?" And again, he says, "I have seen through him."]

Yamada Roshi adds:

... 32 people had accompanied Manjusri on his visit and ... each of them had presented his view on what was involved in the Bodhisattva's entering the Dharma Gate of Non-Duality. The last to speak was Manjusri ... He then asks Vimalakirti to offer his view. Nothing more appears in the koan about how Vimalakirti answered. In the Vimalakirti Sutra, however, it says that Vimalakirti just sat there in silence ... Then Setcho [Hseuh-to] asks us, "What did Vimalakirti say?" ... The *Vimalakirti Sutra* also says that Vimalakirti's silence was like thunder. In his silence, Vimalakirti presents the entire universe ... With his question, [Hseuh-to] shows how he is aware that Vimalakirti ... is perfectly expressing the world of oneness.

From unpublished talks on the *Blue Cliff Record* [*Hekigan roku*]

From the perspective of non-duality, of prajna, of our own vast, empty of self-centeredness, wisdom nature, of Manjusri him or herself, we do not even possess eye ear nose tongue body mind, color sound smell taste touch or what the mind takes hold of. No mind, nothing to gain and no one to gain—or lose—a thing. No wisdom to attain. Or lose. No lion to ride, no sword to swing, and no one to do the riding or wielding. Not this, not that. The sword cuts, the lion leaps, and always present wisdom reveals itself. How can you attain what you already have? Who is there to be, or become, wise?

Thoughts of selflessness can seem threatening to our habitually self-invested self. But "forgetting the self," as Zen Master Dogen termed it, is not a matter of avoiding emotions or side-stepping individuality. Rather, it is like seeing a golden sunrise or a star-filled night and, awed, momentarily forgetting ... ourselves. Such selflessness is like coming home. You step inside, take off your coat, hang up your hat, and rub your hands together, completely at ease. Clinging to thoughts of me, myself, and I never seems to bring us the joy or security we hope for. Aren't our best moments those in which we've been able to forget ourselves? A child walks into the room and our heart opens. A glorious sunset stretches across the twilight, a mountain's peak emerges from the clouds, the taste of tea awakens our tongue and we ourselves are momentarily ... *gone*. Zen's wisdom is to help us live such a self-forgotten, ordinary life. There is a kind of wonder to it—no small thing in itself. Laurens van der Post, upon returning to the big cities of South Africa after his time in the Kalahari among the San (Bushmen) wrote:

> It might sound vague ... but it was clear to me and of the most urgent practical importance to turn back to what we had left of the capacity for wonder. Only reverence for life could deliver us from our inhumanity ... , and from the cataclysm of violence awaiting us at the end of our present road. (*Heart of the Hunter*)

Though he was at the time speaking of the particularly volatile complexities of South Africa and apartheid we're all, to one degree or another, partakers of the same mess. Cutting to the chase, contemporary American Zen teacher, John Daido Loori, would tell his students to "be what you do." The essence of the Buddha Way lies in these simple words, a matter of no longer standing apart as if we were some sort of isolated observer or visitor to life. Roshi Kapleau used to sum up the kind of ordinary alienation that's sadly become the familiar ground of Western feeling and thought by quoting the words of a poem by A.E. Houseman—"I, a stranger and afraid in world I never made."

Dogen, that brilliant, early 13th century teacher, revered as the founder of Japanese Soto Zen, says that to move the self forward to become one with the 10,000 things is called delusion. But to let the 10,000 things come forward to realize themselves as the Self, is intimacy or realization. When the so-called 10,000 things no longer stand "out there," separate from us, either threatening or desirable, we are intimate. Then nothing is a stranger. We find ourselves sitting by the glowing coals of our own hearth. The *Prajna Paramita Hridaya, Heart of Perfect Wisdom*, speaks of the Bodhisattva of Compassion (Avalokitesvara). But Manjusri loves the *Heart* of Perfect Wisdom for it is truly his own heart: Form is only emptiness, emptiness only form.

Perfect wisdom is *revealed*. It is not added to us and cannot be gained. The sword of practice cuts through habits of delusive thinking, allowing the wisdom-that-has-always-been to appear. Seeing colors with the eyes, hearing sounds with the ears, thinking thoughts with the brain, no additional effort is required. We do not need to climb a ladder of thought to get to this. It is ours from before we take our first step up on the first rung of the ladder of thought. It is what that ladder stands on.

Still, when you look through Zen's Gateless Gate, do you think you'll see Manjusri riding a lion? In ancient China a teacher saw an image of Manjusri appearing in the steam rising from the pot of rice he was cooking on the monastery stove. Immediately he hit at it with his spoon to drive it away. This was Manjusri attending to Manjusri.

With a swing of his sword that cuts in One, Manjusri banishes relative realities. Each thing is no longer seen *relatively*, that is, only in relation to other things. Mt. Wutai—the mountain in China sacred to Manjusri—was portrayed as a realm of gold. Everything there, just as it was, was of immeasurable value, an apple of no less worth than a diamond. With no judging of one thing in comparison to another, each thing emerged as unimaginably itself.

The Japanese monk, Ennin, after making the difficult sea voyage to China in 838 CE, went to Mt. Wutai. He then brought the cult of Manjusri back to Japan with him when he returned in 847. In his journals, Ennin wrote of balls of light that moved purposefully among Wu-tai's five peaks, and of pilgrims who gathered nightly there to watch and venerate this manifestation of the bodhisattva. (Ray Bradbury, in *The Martian Chronicles*, wrote of ancient Martians who, having long ago transcended physical matter, appeared as intelligent balls of light to the Earthly missionaries who'd come to Mars to convert the heathen Martians, and who found themselves awed into humility instead.) Ennin wrote, too, of vegetarian feasts on Mt. Wutai, in which food was offered equally to everyone, not just to ordained clergy. Why? Because years earlier, he was told, a pregnant woman at such a feast had demanded double portions—one for herself and one for her unborn child. Her request refused, she rose into the air, became the Bodhisattva Manjusri, and vanished in a blaze of light. After that, all guests on Mt. Wutai were welcomed equally.

The cult of Manjusri was important to lay Buddhists in Tang Era China, as it was in Japan after Ennin brought it there. Which makes sense. Who needs wisdom *more* than lay people who are never off the hook. *The Sutra on Upaseka Precepts*—a sutra on and about lay precepts—says that because lay practice is so difficult, when a lay person arouses the aspiration for enlightenment, "the Four Heavenly Kings and kings of the Akanistha and other heavens pleasantly and with great surprise exclaim, 'Now we have a teacher of men and gods.'"

In Zen, intimacy and enlightenment mean the same thing. Practicing to "get enlightened" is misleading. Can you *get* intimacy? Through ongoing daily practice and periodic sesshin (silent Zen retreats), we begin to see through old habits of un-enlightenment, and become intimate with each thought, emotion, person, tree, or cloud. This is where and how Manjusri's lion roars, and how the lotus, with the book of wisdom on it, blossoms. (Why a lotus? Lotus blossoms rise out of mud, continue through murky water, and finally emerge into air and sunlight where they open fully —an ancient image of life's journey from primal ignorance to spiritual fulfillment.)

The fundamental delusion of duality grows out of habitual belief in the reality of an isolated me "in here," and everything and everyone else, "out there." When Manjusri's sword cuts, all that's *Gone*. Practicing this breath-count, *one* ... *two* and so on, experiencing this breath, absorbing ourselves in a koan point, is how we wield that sword. Without intimacy, we stumble unconsciously through life like so many tourists to the planet, polluting the air and water we need to live, killing plants and animals that are our ancestors and relatives, warring against brothers and sisters. Zen practice is a corrective, but not, alas, a quick fix, and Manjusri is our ally and our guide in this important work.

The word "buddha" may spring from the same root as "to bud." Anyone realizing the intimate wisdom of Manjusri, teacher of buddhas, is then a "budded" being, a lotus heading up through murky water toward sunlight.

3

Meeting Manjusri, Bodhisattva of Wisdom, Face-to-Face

As we will be meeting the Bodhisattvas Manjusri, Kannon, and Maitreya face to face through koans in the next chapters, here's something to keep in mind about koans: while deeply serious, they're also funny in an odd, insightful, freeing sort of way. They can be as topsy-turvy as a Chagall painting, in which lovers float through the air, and a many-colored, transparent goat contains a village. Realities open, settled ground shifts, and odd things happen: a flower is a Dharma teaching; a finger reveals Ultimate Truth; a branch of coral upholds the moon. Zen is not averse to laughter.

> All real laughter, all laughter from the belly, is to some extent a realization of truth, truth that the normal mind with its diffused consciousness and prominent intellectuality can not only never attain, but can and does continually avoid or obscure. The strange thing is that this world which we wish to be free from, is yet the one that we really desire to live in, somehow or other. And when you come to think of it, is not the strength of the paroxysm of delight (we even speak of a man "dying of laughter") that we have in jokes and wit, an evidence that we are momentarily enlightened Buddhas, raised above morality and religion, beyond life and death, into a timeless, spaceless realm that overflows with perpetual happiness, which is nevertheless this world of hopes and fears, remorse and apprehension?
> R.H. Blyth, *Haiku, Vol 1: Eastern Culture.*

And:

> However, a good laugh is a mighty good thing, and rather too scarce a good thing; the more's the pity ... the man that has anything bountifully laughable about him, be sure there is more in that man than you perhaps think ...
> Herman Melville, *Moby Dick*

And:

> If you wish to glimpse inside a human soul and get to know a man ... just watch him laugh. If he laughs well, he's a good man.
> Fyodor Dostoevsky, *The Adolescent*

If it laughs well, it's also likely to be a good spiritual tradition.

Here's what Pulitzer-prize winning poet, environmentalist, and Zen elder Gary Snyder has said about koans:

> The intention of a koan is to make people who are bright in an ordinary way, or ordinary people who are bright in an odd way, work harder and go further into themselves. The language presents an opportunity to perceive a metaphor that calls one not to "thought" but to work. Work is performance. Performance is embodiment, and not subject to ordinary rational analysis—it must spring forth freely and spontaneously, as does life for most working people, who are always dealing with the immediate. That's one kind of koan. So in a way we're not talking about "language," we're talking about the theater of life.

For this to actually work, it needs the relation of student and mentor, in this case a qualified Zen Roshi in the Rinzai tradition. Going into the teacher's room and trying out your view of the koan on him or her is the only way to move through it. Without the mentor, you only dig yourself deeper into the hole, or you make up your own answer, which is invariably wrong.

This remarkable practice, developed and handed down for 1,000 years and more, is very refined and does not fit any exact paradigm of philosophy, rational analysis, or aesthetic strategy. Yet it throws light on them all.

I have no doubt that the Buddhist teachings are grounded in the remarkable, almost unique, exquisitely relevant insights of Gautama Shakyamuni, who is well-named "the Buddha," the realized one. The koans—also known as the kungan, public cases, or teaching phrases—of Chan / Zen Buddhist practice go back to his mind and his insight.

Interview, May 28, 2008, Poetry Foundation

The Blue Cliff Record, (*Hekigan roku* in Japanese), is a collection of 100 koan cases, each with an accompanying introduction, poem, and commentary, put into finished form by Master Yuan-wu (Engo) in 1052, though begun some 60 years earlier by Master Hsueh-tou (Setcho). Zen students in the Harada-Yasutani koan line, which is the koan curriculum I teach, work on the cases of the *Blue Cliff Record* after completing those of the *Gateless Barrier* (*Wu-men kuan* in Chinese, *Mumonkan* in Japanese). Case 35 of the *Blue Cliff Record*, "Manjusri's Threes and Threes," goes like this:

Manjusri asked Wu Cho, "Where have you just come from?"

Wu Cho replied, "The south."

Manjusri said, "How is southern Buddhism faring?"

Wu Cho answered, "The monks of the latter days of the Law have little regard for the precepts."

Manjusri said, "Are there many or few?"

Wu Cho said, "Here about 300, there around 500."

Wu Cho then asked Manjusri, "How does Buddhism fare in this part of the world?"

Manjusri said, "The worldly and the holy dwell together; dragons and snakes intermingle."

Wu Cho asked, "Are there few or many?"

Manjusri said, "In front, three by three; in back, three by three."

What's going on? While wisdom may speak great truths in riddles, it can also hide behind gibberish. Have we been duped?

We seem to live in two worlds, one of ordinary problems, difficulties, and confusions, the other of peace, love, and truth. How painful the one and how wonderful seeming the other. Who wouldn't want to escape from the complexities of the first to arrive in the haven of the second? But must we live divided lives, unhappy *here*, yearning for *there*, even if that wonderful *there* is now called "enlightenment"?

The "latter days of the Law" is a reference to the classical Buddhist belief known as the *mappo*, or Dharma Ending Age. This belief held that access to the True Dharma (i.e. enlightenment) would persist for only 500 years after the Buddha's death or parinirvana. If you practiced sincerely in that period you would awaken. Then, for the next 1,000 years, enlightenment would no longer be "in the bag" even for those who practiced sincerely. For 10,000 years after this (this final period to begin around the year 1,000 CE), enlightenment would remain only as a lovely but distant ideal.

On this timeline the *mappo* or Dharma Ending Age would have begun toward the end of the Tang Dynasty, the so-called "Golden Age of Zen" and the start of the Song Dynasty, which, ironically, is when the *Blue Cliff Record* and *Gateless Barrier* were created and the practice of realization—the heart of Zen tradition—was in full swing. The koan takes this deeply pessimistic idea, and in a kind of spiritual judo, flips it over, so that Manjusri's timeless wisdom can emerge.

Still, the essential point, that it's hard to keep the real thing going when your times are not supportive, is hard to dismiss. Wars, pandemics, financial disruption, political corruption, environmental chaos, famine and drought create deep anxieties that, willy-nilly, push us toward self-protective thought and behavior. Then fame, power, and wealth are going to look like our best hedges against the constant sense of threat. In such a dog-eat-dog world, looking out for number one gets baked in. And yet, because things are so difficult, in such times a willingness to take risks and see for ourselves if there might not be something "more," can also emerge. What have we got to lose? As always, it's the best of times, the worst of times, in this tale not just of two cities, but of two realities.

Here's the case with some added personal commentary:

Manjusri asked Wu Cho, "Where have you just come from?" What's he getting at?

Wu Cho replied, "The south." Admirably honest, but has the pilgrim floundered?

Manjusri said, "How is southern Buddhism faring?" The Bodhisattva ambles down the mountain.

Wu Cho answered, "The monks of the latter days of the Law [Dharma] have little regard for the precepts." Tough times. Wu Cho is an honest man.

Manjusri said, "Are there many or few?" What difference do numbers make? Maybe a lot, maybe none at all. If many, how many? Is anyone left out? If few, how few? Is there even one? Leaving aside thoughts of many or few, how's *your* practice going?

Wu Cho said, "Here about 300, there around 500." Honest to a fault, but as numbers go it's not bad. Perhaps others may join in. There's security in numbers. Then again, "Bodhidharma had only one disciple, and even he was a cripple." (*Gateless Barrier*, Case 41) What number are you?

Wu Cho then asked Manjusri, "How does Buddhism fare in this part of the world?" Turning the spear point, he puts Manjusri on the spot. What part of the world is "this part"? By the way, Wu Cho—as we'll see—never knew he was talking with Manjusri. The case sees through the mask.

Manjusri said, "The worldly and the holy dwell together; dragons and snakes intermingle." What kind of world is this? We have dictators and Dalai Lamas, Black Widow spiders and emotional-support dogs? Manjusri, tells it like it is. Does anyone understand?

Wu Cho asked, "Are there few or many?" He repeats Manjusri's question, exposing himself to the return arrow.

Manjusri said, "In front, three by three; in back, three by three." Bullseye! The set-up pays off. It can't be grasped. There's no place to take hold. Gone-beyond wisdom is inaccessible to reason. Or is Manjusri just babbling? We must realize the meaning, not imitate the illogic.

Yuan-wu's commentary—a thousand year-old Extended Director's Cut—reveals both backstory and aftermath. The essence is that Wu Cho, a Buddhist pilgrim to Mt. Wu Tai, got lost at night on the mountainside. Then Manjusri created an illusory temple for the lost pilgrim to take shelter in, and taking the form himself of an old man like the temple grounds-keeper, approached and asked, "Where have you come from?" thereby initiating the dialog of the koan. Later, when they had tea together, the old man held up a crystal bowl or cup and asked, "Do they also have this in the South?" Wu Cho said, "No." "Then what do they drink tea from?" said the old man, a response that left Wu Cho speechless. Perhaps he was starting to sense that something unusual was going on.

In the morning, the old man directed a young attendant to show their guest out to the temple gate. Wu Cho asked the boy "The old man said, 'In front three by three; in back three by three.' How many is this?" The boy responded, "Oh Worthy!" Wu Cho said, "Yes?" The boy said, "How many is this?"(The sharp-witted boy is also Manjusri.) Wu Cho asked, "What temple is this?" The boy pointed to the guardian figures at the temple entrance. When Wu Cho turned to look, the temple and the boy both vanished. Wu Cho found himself alone in an empty valley, the vast empty sky above, and the towering crags of the blue mountains his only actual companions.

Later, Wu Cho was cook at a temple on Mt. Wutai—an important position reserved for senior monks, as the community's health depended on the cook's attention and virtue. When he was preparing rice, Manjusri would sometimes appear as a vision in the steam rising from the pot. When it happened, Wu Cho would hit at the apparition with his wooden spoon to drive it away. Clearly, he had matured.

The unique genius of Zen is on full display in this koan. In it a complex visionary event is condensed down into something personal and intimate. Zen delights in taking episodes of Buddhist vision and myth, entire chapters of sutras, and turning them into concise koans. We see this same process of empowerment at work, this same delight in condensation and miniaturization unfolding throughout history, when the structures of large, community-wide ceremonies are absorbed into oral tales and eventually, from there, are recreated as written literature, texts that can be carried and transported but still retain a power to change, move, and even transform us. We see this in our lives today, when room-sized computers are condensed down into even more powerful cellphones—a process we should expect to continue as quantum computers appear on the scene.

Koans, we might say, are the cell phones of myth. The power of the larger structure is still there, alive in the koan, but amplified by its process of condensation. The ancient truth, that power dwells in the smallest things, seems almost hard for us to miss these days, living as we do with $E=mc^2$, the silicon chip, and with our expanding knowledge of the immense library stored in the spiraling of our DNA.

Still, belief in the mappo can't simply be ignored as so much superstition. It, too, emerges from something truthful. Progress is never one way. What has been lost along the way? Not to overly romanticize things, there was a time when human beings lived in greater harmony with and awareness of the living Earth, and human communities fostered spiritual growth and maturity as the way of the human being. Ceremonies, vision quests, and pilgrimages were part of all our ancestors' lives. These days we are on our own, and it's up to each of us to find ways to mature, even as our times are making it abundantly clear that our immaturity is killing us and our world. One problem, of course, is that we also know that, even if we do our best, we can still end up feeling anxious, even hopeless. The more aware we become the more problems we uncover, and, so, the worse we can feel. Doing our best, then, can look like doing very little. This is our own version of living in the *mappo*.

So greater numbers can, indeed, feel encouraging, providing us with a degree of hope that we'll reach a tipping point. Plus, it's a relief to feel we're not alone. Long ago I was in a workshop given by poet and "men's movement" leader, Robert Bly. He said—and rightly so—"Having companions increases our courage." This is good to know, and is the foundation of sangha, of working together for good and meaningful and compassionate goals. But there's also something about numbers that's not quite so straightforward. The greater the number of people involved, the greater the need for organizational structures. Hierarchies and bureaucracies, and forms and systems can become thought of as *the teaching*. We take less personal responsibility in groups, and giving away our power, become small. The traditional advice for teisho (a Zen talk by the teacher; not so much a lecture as a teacher's presentation *of* Zen) is to listen as if the talk were directed to you *alone*, as if no one else was there, and you were only the recipient. Such aloneness has nothing to do with loneliness. Rather it is empowering. So, there is a danger in numbers. More can be less and, less, more.

While there is One reality (can there be two?), in this koan we meet with two radically different versions of it. In the one, a number of people are practicing and doing their best. In the other, there's no way to grasp or count, no way to know how it's going, so what numbers and what Dharma-ending Age are you even talking about? Is this ordinary life holy or worldly? If saints and sinners, fire-breathing dragon-like practitioners, and ordinary garden variety sitters intermingle, how can we tell which is which? Are there many or few? Yamada Roshi writes, "Think of a public bath in traditional Japan – stripped of everything and all in it together! How's that for 'The worldly and saints live together, dragons and snakes are mixed with each other.'"

The koan says that even when things don't seem to be going well, Original Mind and the realization of it, this True World world as seen by and as the wisdom of Manjusri, is always accessible. Which doesn't mean it will be easy. Times can be hard and such times can make this possibility seem— and feel—impossibly far off, chimerical and distant. But, says this koan, the possibility of realization, of entrance into Manjusri's insight is always there. A hopeful message, indeed.

When Wu Cho first visited Mt. Wu Tai, spoke with Manjusri, and was later shown out, he looked back and saw *nothing*, just an empty valley and overarching sky. Appearances can be deceptive. Maybe *this* was his big moment, his real meeting with Manjusri. *Nothing at all.* In the *Transmission of the Lamp*, biographies of Zen ancestors compiled around the year 1,000, Feng-kan, a Zen Master who was said to ride tigers, also met with an old man up on Mt. Wu Tai. During his encounter, Feng-asked the old man directly if he might not be Manjusri. The old man answered, "Can there be two Manjusris?" It's said that upon hearing this response Feng-kan immediately bowed. But by the time he straightened from his bow, the old man had vanished.

Then again, when Wu Cho, in our koan case, was sheltered in the illusory temple and spoke with an old man who was Manjusri and a boy attendant (who was also Manjusri), wasn't it real to him? Weren't these events as real for Wu Cho as the events of our own lives? And yet there was—nothing. Though this is not a point in the koan, it touches something worth exploring, nonetheless. And, yet, Manjusri's "3x3 front, 3x3 back," is the truly intimate point. Through it, like Wu Cho, we, too, can meet the Bodhisattva face-to-face.

There are religions that claim we can move from this present world of trials and challenges and, by leading "good" lives here will, after death, find ourselves in heaven, where we will undoubtedly receive fulfillment and reward. But let me ask: do we really want to wait until our actual life is over to discover if this is true or not? And what kind of life or world might this create? Perhaps the very kind of world we have; a world seen as a mere way station to something better; a disposable and, so, uncared for, world. Perhaps it leads to the very difficulties and problems we now globally face and know too well. And what if, sadly, all of it springs from a mistake in how we understand—and use—our own minds? Manjusri says we can do better.

How shall we live in this place of challenge and difficulty and find satisfaction, meaning, and joy right where we actually are? How is this difficult world the very place we seek? This is the assurance of Zen master Hakuin's *Zazen Wasan, Song in Praise of Zazen* which concludes: "This place where we stand is the pure lotus land/and this very body, the body of Buddha." Given what we see and deal with every day, how can this be? Was even the great teacher, Hakuin, wearing rose-colored glasses? *Case 37 of the Book of Serenity (Shoyoroku).* "Kuei-shan's (Isan's) Karmic Consciousness" puts it like this:

> Kuei-shan asked Yang-shan, "Suppose a man asks you, 'How about one who says all sentient beings are in a disorderly karmic consciousness and have no base to rely upon.' How would you treat him?"
>
> Yang-shan said, "If a man appears, I call to him. When he turns his head, instantly I say, 'What is that?' I wait while he hesitates, and then I say to him, 'There is not only disorderly karmic consciousness, but there is no base to rely upon.'"
>
> Keui-shan said, "Oh, good."

In "Genesis," the Creator brings forth night and day, arranges the heavens, produces the sun, moon, and Earth with its many fruit-bearing trees and countless living beings, and at each advancing stage of Creation we hear something very much like this same, "Oh, good!"

Right here, where East and West seem to fundamentally agree, might be a good place to take our stand and find out what such "goodness" really means.

Manjusri's, "three by three front, three by three back," might be a very *good* place to start.

4

Manjusri Fails: A Woman Comes Out of Meditation

Case 42 of *The Gateless Barrier*, which also features Manjusri, takes a seemingly odd turn. In it, the great and powerful Bodhisattva of Wisdom, in a classic Wizard of Oz scenario, ("ignore that man behind the curtain"), stands exposed as neither wise nor powerful. The koan, which opens in a realm of myth, returns us to our ordinary world, now a world transformed. Here's the case, sometimes also called "Manjusri and the Young Woman in Samadhi."

> Once Manjusri went to a place where many Buddhas had assembled with the World-Honored One. When he arrived, all the Buddhas had returned to their original dwelling place. Only a young woman remained, seated in samadhi, near the Buddha's seat.
> Manjusri addressed the Buddha and asked, "How can the young woman get near the Buddha's seat when I cannot?"
> The Buddha replied to Manjusri, "Awaken this young woman from her samadhi and ask her yourself!" Manjusri walked around the young woman three times, snapped his fingers once, took her to the Brahma Heaven and exerted all his supernatural powers, but he could not bring her out.
> The World-Honored One said, "Even a hundred thousand Manjusris cannot awaken her. Down below, past twelve hundred million lands, as innumerable as the

sands of the Ganges, lives the Bodhisattva of Delusive Wisdom, in the early stages of practice. He will be able to bring her out of her samadhi."

Instantly the Bodhisattva of Delusive Wisdom emerged from the earth and made bows before the World-Honored One, who gave his imperial order. Delusive Wisdom stepped before the young woman, snapped his fingers once, and at this she came out of samadhi.

Wu-men's Commentary:

The comedy Old Shakya puts on the stage here is a great hodgepodge. Just tell me now; Manjusri is the teacher of the Seven Buddhas – why couldn't he get the young woman out of her samadhi, when the Bodhisattva of Delusive Wisdom, a beginner, could? If you can firmly grasp this point, then for you this busy life of ignorance and discrimination will be the life of the Dragon Samadhi.

Wu-men's Verse:

One can awaken her, the other cannot;
Both of them are free.
A god mask, a devil mask
The failure is wonderful indeed.

Note: the name, "Bodhisattva of Delusive Wisdom," is Robert Aitken Roshi's translation. Other English versions name him, "Momyo." But Aitken Roshi has kindly sharpened the case for us.

What is this gathering about? Most likely, Buddhas have come from across the universe to brainstorm their essential task: how to liberate suffering beings. So they've come to talk shop. This story of their meeting and of Manjusri's late arrival, appears in a sutra titled, *The Collected Essentials of All Buddhas*, in which the Buddha-gathering is revealed to have taken place in a distant galaxy named "The Buddha Land of Tenno Tathagatha." Here, that vast cosmic event simply forms the backdrop to the koan proper.

Sutras say that our universe is filled with innumerable worlds and countless Buddhas, and that incomprehensible periods of time have already passed between the arising of Buddha after Buddha right here on Earth, where Zen tradition honors seven such fully awakened beings, Shakyamuni Buddha being the latest and most recent.

The koan makes use of the larger, epic story in order to challenge us to actually awaken ourselves and realize Manjusri's intimately non-dual, selfless wisdom. And, through the intricacies of the koan, come to understand the fundamental nature of our own lives and daily reality. Though it's a play—as Wu-men, compiler of the *Gateless Barrier* takes pains to point out—it's not the kind of performance we can simply enjoy from our seats. It's truth won't open to us so passively. We can't just applaud at the end and leave the theater. Instead, we ourselves must get up onto the stage and join in the drama. The koan is as participatory as the Living Theater of the '60s. No mere observers! Participants all! Life itself is performative, after all.

And what a show it is! The curtain rises as Manjusri is being admitted to the gathering—only to discover that all the Buddhas have already returned to their "original dwelling place." Why? And where is that place?" As a, perhaps, interesting side-note to this dramatic opening scene, Master Wu-men here and, indeed, throughout his *Gateless Barrier*, reminds me of Bob Dylan, for—

> We are celebrating an artist who can transform his personal experience into something mythic and then

back again into something that is personally meaningful to his listener. (This double operation is at the heart of his genius.)

The Guardian, May 22, 2021 – "Bob Dylan at 80: In Praise of a Mighty and Unbowed Singer-songwriter"

The connection may not be far-fetched. Perhaps it is one that Dylan himself recognizes. On Dylan's album, *Rough and Rowdy Ways*, lines like "eye like a shooting star," and "climbed a mountain of swords on bare feet," sound suspiciously like lines lifted directly from the *Gateless Barrier*, specifically Wu-men's commentary to case 8, "Hsi Chung's Carts" which goes, "If you realize this directly, your eye is like a shooting star and your activity like a flash of lightning," and his verse to case 17, "The National Teacher Calls Three Times" which concludes: "If you want to support the gate and sustain the house,/You must climb a mountain of swords with bare feet." Has Dylan been dipping into our venerable Zen text? Was Wu-men the Dylan of his time, and is Dylan the Wu-men of ours?

In any case, speculation aside, Manjusri goes to a gathering of many Buddhas, only to find that all the Buddhas have returned to their original place. Aitken Roshi, in his commentary on the case, says that if you get the why and wherefore of this, the rest of the case will be "in the bag" for you. (*The Gateless Barrier: The Wu-Men Kuan* [Mumonkan], Robert Aitken.) In short, he's telling us that the mythic will have become intimate.

Except not all the Buddhas are gone. Shakyamuni Buddha remains and, oddly, seated close to him, is a young woman deep in samadhi, out beyond her ordinary daily consciousness and seemingly rather stuck there. Why can a young woman sit near the Buddha, when Manjusri, the Buddha's own teacher, can't? Shouldn't the Bodhisattva of Perfect Wisdom be closer to the Buddha than *anyone*? Yet here he is, kept distant from the Buddha, while a young woman, a beginner no less, sits close to him.

This part of the case draws on a dark aspect of both Asian history and the world's. Classical Asian Buddhism, essentially monastic in form, paid little attention to women's abilities and achievements. Though wise women appear in sutras and koans, rarely do we meet with them as Dharma Ancestors, which means as fully acknowledged enlightened teachers. Fortunately this is changing. Contemporary research is reclaiming both the realized ordained and lay women, and lay men, too, who were always there, hidden in the shadows of monastic patriarchy. So a misogynist history lies behind this koan point. It's not simply that an ordinary person is near the Buddha while a great bodhisattva isn't. It's that a young *woman* is there and doing rather well, too, her very youth emphasizing her unworthiness. (In ancient China the elderly received deep respect, not so much the young.) As a woman, she carries as well the stains of menstruation, pregnancy, and projected male desire—all of which would have made this case something of a mind-bender. "What, a young woman is close to the Buddha? Impossible!" Which is disturbingly similar to the hook in the classic koan of "Chao-chou"s Dog," the first koan in *The Gateless Barrier*. Asked by a monk if even something even as *lowly as a dog* has Buddha-nature, master Chao-chou answered "Mu"—a response that has benefited countless Zen practitioners for the last 1,000 years. Our koan of Manjusri and the young woman asks, "Can even someone as *lowly as a young woman* have spiritual potential?" However, this is used by Wu-men in the koan not to uphold misogyny, but to empower the drama. Think of an actor screaming their lines. It's done for emphasis. Wu-men, compiler of *The Gateless Barrier*, used what his culture offered to dramatize the point.

He might also have something up his sleeve. In both the *Lotus Sutra* and the *Vimalakirti Sutra*, a naga princess (in the former), and a youthful goddess (in the latter), put monks and arhats alike to shame with their Buddha wisdom. Perhaps Wu-men is giving a nod to a deeper truth:

practice-realization is open to all, wisdom accessible to everyone. If so, bravo!

Now, about the young woman's condition. The word "samadhi" is from the Sanskrit root, "sam-a-dha," meaning 'to collect' or 'bring together,' and is typically translated as "concentration' or 'unification of mind." In short, it is a condition of the mind absorbed in its own presence, in silent, one-pointed, attention-less attention, a selfless but not necessarily awakened condition. It can be pleasurable, even blissful. However, if we become attached to this condition as more real than our ordinary experience, we can create yet another obstacle. Daily life, haunted by memories of "something more special," can now seem not good enough. Which might be OK as motivation to mature further, knowing deeper living is possible. But if we cling to blissful states and our memories of them, we can get rather stuck. Some people, experiencing a degree of peace through breath practice, can hesitate to take on the challenge of koan practice, fearing it will threaten their "happy enough" condition.

If our aspiration is awakening, then faith is important. Faith in what? Faith in our own nature, and in our own potential to wake to it. Roshi Kapleau used to say that Zen requires only one fundamental article of faith: faith that the Buddha was neither a fool nor a liar when, upon his great enlightenment, to his own astonishment he exclaimed, "Wonder of wonders! All beings are Buddhas, fully endowed with wisdom and virtue. Only their self-centered thinking prevents them from realizing it." At some point, such faith leads us to think, "If the Buddha wasn't a fool or a liar, then what *did* he mean? "All beings" must also mean me. But how can I be a Buddha, filled as I am with confusion, anxiety, anger, jealousy, pettiness? And if we're *all* Buddhas, why all this suffering, why all this injustice and hatred? What's going on? What's at the root?"

Probing into such questions is itself the path of practice-realization. Which might begin years before we ever decide to cross our legs or enter a zendo. Faith and doubt—which does not mean simple skepticism—are not really that different. Doubt is faith in action, faith the foundation of doubt. The doubt that Zen speaks of means openness, wonder, a creative willingness to look directly, not simply accept pre-packaged answers. It frees us to really ask "Why is the world so filled with injustice and difficulty? Who am I? Why was I born? Why am I here? Why must I die? Where are we going?" It is a way of removing blinders, and reclaiming innate freedom. While calm and steadiness are deeply valuable, they are not, in themselves, insight. Which is the point of the koan, of every koan. They are not just pointers toward further practice or subtle concepts. They are, each one, doorways of realization right now.

Why can't the most deeply insightful bodhisattva, the Bodhisattva of Wisdom himself, get close to the Buddha, while someone new, who's not even considered to have much potential, someone rather stuck, too, in an early phase of practice, sits close by him? The koan's initial challenge was, where did the Buddhas go and why? The second is why can't Manjusri get close to the Buddha while a young woman can? It seems crazy, even ridiculous.

That she sits close to the Buddha and he can't really bugs Manjusri. So he asks, "What's going on?" The Buddha answers, "Awaken her and find out yourself." So Manjusri snaps his fingers beside her ear, circumambulates around her, even takes her up to the highest Brahma Heavens, where the heavenly splendor might bring her around, or the terror of looking down from such heights might shock her out of her stuckness.

Nothing works. Manjusri, the great Bodhisattva, teacher of the past seven Buddhas, *fails*. Why? This question, too, demands our personal clarification. Not only can't Manjusri, the wisest of all the great bodhisattva-mahasattvas get close to the Buddha, but he also can't bring this young woman, a beginner, out of her limited samadhi. What gives?

What is the function of wisdom? What is Manjusri's purpose? Why can't he enter the Assembly of Buddhas? Why have all the Buddhas returned to their original place? What is their original place? Why can't Manjusri get close to the Buddha while a young woman can? And, why can't he bring her out of her limited samadhi? And, if all this wasn't enough, there remains a final humiliating twist. After Manjusri fails, a beginner bodhisattva who we're told resides countless worlds, perhaps entire world systems or galaxies away, immediately appears and without hesitation, easily awakens the young woman. *Snap!* Just like that, she emerges from her samadhi. Which concludes the case.

Wu-men himself, compiler of *The Gateless Barrier*, calls this koan a total mishmash, a hodgepodge. And yet, the play's the thing. Here, again, is Wu-men's commentary on it:

> The comedy Old Shakya puts on the stage here is a great hodgepodge. Just tell me now; Manjusri is the teacher of the Seven Buddhas – why couldn't he get the young woman out of her samadhi, when the Bodhisattva of Delusive Wisdom, a beginner, could? If you can firmly grasp this point, then for you this busy life of ignorance and discrimination will be the life of the Dragon Samadhi.

Why does he call it a comedy? What is the essence of the hodgepodge? The pay-off is that if you get clear on this, Wu-men says that for you, this ordinary life with its absurdities, challenges, and injustices; its joys, sorrows, ups and downs, will be the Dragon Samadhi. That is, you won't simply gain a condition of calm, peace, or bliss, or realize some momentary experience of Oneness. Instead, this very life, just as it is, will be transformed into liberation, realization, enlightenment. Like some great dragon, your insight will swallow the universe in a single gulp.

Hold on. Wait. Not so fast. Our ordinary life, with its problems, messes, misunderstandings, disappointments and difficulties will be enlightenment? Our time-factored, limited life, with its failed relationships, missed opportunities, anxieties, injustices, angers, sorrows, and fleeting joys will be the Great Liberation? Really? Wu-men doesn't simply say to have faith in this. He's saying that it's simply so. The carrot is that the Dragon Samadhi sounds like what we're looking for; the stick is that we might make an effort and fail. Kapleau Roshi used to offer these encouraging words: "If you don't let the Dharma down, the Dharma will never let you down." And, "Nothing done sincerely is a wasted effort." In short, virtue is its own reward. "Virtue" needn't mean "goodness." The virtue of iron is strength, the virtue of ice is cold. Practice is its own reward whether we deem it a "success" or not. There is virtue in making a sincere, whole-hearted effort. Wu-men's verse:

> One can awaken her, the other cannot;
> Both of them are free.
> A god mask, a devil mask
> The failure is wonderful indeed.

One can, one can't. Isn't that unfair? Shakespeare was an immediate success, but Melville never received a single positive review on his masterwork, *Moby Dick*. Picasso never failed to receive worshipful accolades, yet Van Gogh never sold a painting and William Blake died in poverty. One can awaken her, the other cannot. Astoundingly, Wu-men asserts that both are free. If so, how is Manjusri free, and how is the Bodhisattva of Delusive Wisdom also free? How is Einstein free and how Walt Disney? And what about us? How are we free, Dragon Samadhi or no? Put on a god mask and people bow in awe. Wear a devil mask and everyone runs away in terror. How often in the course of a single day, might we put on one mask and take off another?

Can failure *be* wonderful indeed? We dread failure, don't we? We want "A"s, not "F"s. In the movie, "The Right Stuff," when Alan Shepard, the first astronaut into space is sealed into his tiny capsule perched at the top of a lethally explodeable rocket, there at the knife-edge of life and death he utters his heartfelt prayer: "Oh, Lord. Don't let me fuck up." He's not asking to survive or to triumph. He's asking not to fail. Is Manjusri's failure "wonderful indeed" or sour grapes? Is the koan saying that in the long run painful experiences are for the best? If so, isn't that a dodge, an "Oh well—good enough"? Wouldn't that be to mistake a bell for a pot, as Wu-men says in another context? Then again a snake's inability to gallop, makes it a truly marvelous snake, not a failed horse. What if having no leg to stand on is our strength?

To know such wonderful failure, we ourselves must awaken to Manjusri's *Nothing-at-All*, the vast wisdom of Just This! in which there is no me, no you, no self, no other. This total failure of all our egotistic stratagems, of all our old ploys and plots, is called "enlightenment." Yet we also live within the wisdom of Momyo, the still wet-behind-the-ears Bodhisattva of Delusive Wisdom. Snapping his fingers, Momyo instantly awakens the young woman—just like that.

Quantum entanglement says that a single molecule or atom, far off on the other side of the universe, will rotate in unison with its twin on this side, no matter the incalculable distances between. The Bodhisattva of Delusive Wisdom and the young woman are an entangled pair. He snaps his fingers and she comes out of her meditation. They "get" each other; speak the same language. Why? How? And why is the great Bodhisattva of Wisdom out in the cold?

In an old Irish tale, the great warrior, poet, shaman, and king, Fionn, challenges his men with the question: "What is the most beautiful music in the world?" They each offer good answers such as: the call of the lark, the laughter of a child, the sigh of a woman, the baying of the hounds, the ringing of sword against shield in battle. Fionn rejects them all. Finally, when his men press him, he says that the most beautiful music in the world is "the music of what happens"—which turns the tale into an Irish koan.

Quantum mechanics tends to agree with Fionn. The micro-second by micro-second unfolding of ordinary daily reality, "the music of what happens," is the result of the failure of all other options. Lines of quantum possibility extending micro-second by micro-second in all directions, collapse into the single line we rather naively (and, perhaps, recklessly) call "reality." All other possible lines of existence are no-shows, failures. The taste of this tea, the pink of these blossoms, the *Caw*! of this crow—the failure is certainly wonderful indeed! But what about the tragic, painful, and terrible things that happen? Are they, too, "wonderful indeed"? Here's where it gets sticky. To fall into a concept about it, to generalize won't hold up. Job was only fully answered by the Voice out of the Whirlwind. The consolation of philosophy—any philosophy, any concept—deconstructs in the end. What is this failure that is wonderful indeed?

It's hard not to fall into thinking of Zen practice-realization in terms of winning and losing, attaining and failing. When we're passed on a koan, we can think, "Bravo, success!" and feel great. When stuck on a koan or rung out of the dokusan room, we can feel like a failure. Is any of it relevant? Is enlightenment our greatest success or greatest failure? Bob Dylan says, "There's no success like failure, and failure's no success at all." ("Love Minus Zero/No Limit.") Roshi Kapleau used to ask at workshops, "If you have an alcohol problem who might help you more—a therapist or a reformed alcoholic?" Then, he would answer saying, "Both. They both could help, each in their own way." Contemporary Zen teachers, looking at this koan of Manjusri, Momyo, and the young woman, say: "Think of flying a modern jet plane. A hundred thousand Manjusris probably couldn't start and fly it. But an ordinary jet pilot can do it easily."

Manjusri, the great Wisdom Bodhisattva and Momyo, the Bodhisattva of Delusive Wisdom, like the Delusive Wisdom Bodhisattva and the young woman, also form a pair. Manjusri can't do anything without Momyo; Momyo has no essential wisdom without Manjusri. What is the difference between their two kinds of wisdom? And as a final challenge to our hodgepodge of a comedy, whose wisdom is the greater, Manjusri's or Momyo's?

Though this may be off topic, here's a story: Back in the 60s, Danan Henry Roshi had an old VW bus. One night as he was driving along a lonely rural road, the bus broke down. Cursing and grumbling, he started walking toward the lights of a farmhouse twinkling a mile or so ahead. As he walked along the empty road the odors of trees and plants, of field and forest came to him on soft night breezes. The Milky Way rippled and shone overhead. It became one of the most beautiful walks and memorable nights of his life. Wonderful! Wonderful failure, indeed!

Turning again to Bob Dylan, the erstwhile failed iron country Minnesotan formerly known as Robert Zimmerman, "Right now I can't read so good, don't send me no more letters, no./ Not unless you mail them from Desolation Row."

5

The Bodhisattva of Great Compassion: Kannon, Kanjizai, Kwan-Yin, Avalokitesvara

Emperor Wu of Liang asked the Great Master Bodhidharma, "What is the first principle of the holy teachings?"

Bodhidharma said, "Emptiness without holiness."

The Emperor said, "Who is standing before me?"

Bodhidharma replied, "I don't know."

The Emperor did not understand. Thereupon Bodhidharma crossed the Yangtse River and came to the kingdom of Wei.

Later the Emperor brought this up to the Prince Chih, who asked, "Does your Majesty know who this man is?" The Emperor said, "I don't know." Prince Chih said, "He is the Bodhisattva Avalokiteshvara transmitting the Buddha Mind Seal." The Emperor felt regretful and wanted to send an emissary to invite Bodhidharma to return. Prince Chih told him, "Your Majesty, it is no good

[65]

sending a messenger to fetch him back. Even if everyone in the whole country were to go after him, he still would not return."

Case 1, *Blue Cliff Record*

Asked to write something about the Bodhisattva of Great Compassion, Hakuin penned, "Even if the rivers and seas all receded and became dry land/ Her vow to save all sentient beings still would never cease." (*Complete Poison Blossoms from A Thicket of Thorn*). In other words, even if the world turned upside down, and seas became mountains and mountains, seas (which has happened), even then, the Bodhisattva of Great Compassion will not think only of herself and her own needs, but would remain ever dedicated to the welfare of all.

It's quite a statement. Even in moments of the greatest possible panic and self-concern, even in moments of absolute catastrophe when all our cherished beliefs, all our sense of security is gone, even then, for the Bodhisattva, compassion is primary. Such selflessness is not a matter of will, but of love, a word which, while rarely used in Zen, is very much about what's actually there, underlying everything. Talking about love, about G-d, has built-in consequences. Sometimes talk cheapens what we care most about, and makes us way too glib. Actions, as the old saying goes, speak louder than words. The Bodhisattva of Compassion knows this truth well.

Three archetypal images may be said to sum up Zen practice. First is the historic Buddha, who 2500 years ago, sat beneath the Bodhi-tree, transcended self-centeredness, and touching the Earth, fully Awoke, opening the Way and setting the Dharma Wheel in motion. Second is Manjusri, teacher of the past seven Buddhas, opening the way of actual practice-realization for us all, being both the activity *of* practice as well as the vast empty nature that is no-nature, which is the birthright of all. Third is Avalokitesvara, Bodhisattva of Compassion, Hearer of the

The Bodhisattva of Great Compassion

Cries of the World and responder, too, bringer of the healing balm of skillfully applied compassion to all suffering beings. She is emptiness itself as action, as form. Blake wrote "Eternity is in love with the productions of time." (*The Marriage of Heaven and Hell.*) The realization of this is Manjusri; the un-self-centered expression of that realization is Avalokitesvara.

The Lotus Sutra's 25th chapter, the major section of which is chanted regularly in Zen monasteries, is dedicated to the saving power of Avalokitesvara. In this section of the sutra the bodhisattva frees devotees from every imaginable form of suffering and every possible disaster—fires, floods, famine, beasts, torture, prisons, droughts, swords, and shipwreck. Supposedly not long before his death, Zen Master Dogen walked around his quarters in kinhin ("sutra walking"—walking while maintaining a mind focused on the practice) reciting this section of the *Lotus Sutra*. A chanted version, used at the Vermont Zen Center, in which the Bodhisattva is identified as Kanzeon, is as follows:

The *Lotus Sutra* Scripture of Kanzeon Bodhisattva

Leader:
    In verse Mujinni Bodhisattva asked,
    "World Honored One possessor of all grace
    For what reason is the heir of the Buddha named Kanzeon?"
All:
    The World Honored One answered too in verse:
    "Listen to the actions of Kanzeon
    Which have their application to all!
    Her vow is deep like the ocean
    Unfathomable though kalpas pass
    A myriad of Buddhas she has truly served

And made a great, pure vow.
If you hear her name and see her body,
and bear her in mind,
Your life will not be in vain;
And you will end all sufferings.
If someone wants to hurt you
And pushes you into a great firepit,
If you think on the power of Kanzeon
The firepit will change into a pond.
If you're cast adrift upon the vast ocean
And meet danger from dragons, fish and demons,
If you think on the power of Kanzeon
The waves will not drown you.
If from the peak of Sumeru
Someone would push you down
If you think on the power of Kanzeon
Like the sun you will stand firm in the sky.
If evil ones chase you
And push you from Mount Diamond,
If you think on the power of Kanzeon
Not even a single hair will be harmed.
If robbers surround you
Each with a sword drawn to strike,
If you think on the power of Kanzeon
Compassion will awaken in them.
If you suffer by royal command
And your life is to end in execution,
If you think on the power of Kanzeon
The sword will be broken to bits.
If you are imprisoned,
Shackled, and chained,

The Bodhisattva of Great Compassion

If you think on the power of Kanzeon
The fetters will drop and you'll be released.
If someone wants to injure you
With curses or poison,
If you think on the power of Kanzeon
These ills will return from whence they came.
If you meet evil rakshas,
Poisonous dragons or demons,
If you think on the power of Kanzeon
They will not dare to harm you.
If you are surrounded by evil beasts
Whose teeth and claws are fearfully sharp
If you think on the power of Kanzeon
They will run away in boundless retreat.
If vipers, lizards, snakes or scorpions,
Threaten to scorch you with poisonous breath
If you think on the power of Kanzeon
They will turn away quickly at the sound
of your voice.
If clouds thunder and lightning flashes,
If hailstones beat and rain pours down,
If you think on the power of Kanzeon
Immediately they will vanish away.
If sentient beings are in great adversity
And immeasurable suffering presses them down,
The wonderful power of the wisdom of Kannon can
relieve the sufferings of the world.
Endowed with transcendent powers
Full master of wisdom and skillful means,
In all the worlds in the ten directions,
There's no place she doesn't manifest herself.

The suff'rings of those in the troubled states:
Hell dwellers, hungry spirits, and beasts;
The sufferings of birth, old age, illness and death all
by degrees are ended by her.
She of the true gaze, she of the pure gaze,
gaze of great and encompassing wisdom,
gaze of pity, gaze of compassion—
ever longed for, ever revered.
She is a spotless pure ray of light,
A sun of wisdom dispelling darkness.
Subduer of woes of storm and fire
Illumining all the world.
Her will of compassion shakes like thunder;
Her mind of mercy is like a great cloud
Which sends down sweet dew of Dharma rain to
quench the flames of earthly desires.
In disputes before judges or in the midst of battle,
If you think on the power of Kanzeon
All enemies will flee away.
She has a wondrous voice,
The voice of one who perceives the world,
A brahma voice, voice of the rolling tide,
A voice unsurpassed in all this world;
Therefore you should always think on her.
Have no doubt, even for a moment
The pure seer Kanzeon will be a refuge
When suffering distress or the misery of death. She
is endowed with every quality.
Her eye of compassion views all sentient beings, her
ocean of blessings is beyond measure. Therefore
you should pay homage to her."

The Bodhisattva of Great Compassion

Then Jiji bodhisattva arose,
Stood before the Buddha and addressed him thus:
"World Honored One, they who hear this scripture
Of Kanzeon bosatsu, and hear of her deeds
And transcendent powers,
No small amount of merit will they gain."
Lead Chanter: *(All with hands in gassho)*
When the Buddha taught the scripture of the life
and work of the All-Sided One, all present then in
number eighty-four thousand strong, with all their
hearts cherished a longing for the Supreme Enlightenment, with which nothing in all the universe
compares.

Iconographically, Avalokitesvara or, Kannon, appears in a variety of forms. She may be seated at ease beside a stream or river, beneath the branches of a willow. She may be standing, looking steadily out at the world and its beings, sometimes while holding a vase or jar filled with healing balm. With the vase upright, healing power is held in readiness; with the vase pointed downward, it is pouring out into the world. Kannon may also hold a scroll, or appear as a fisherman's wife holding a basket. In India, China, and Tibet, as well as in Japan, Avalokitesvara may also often appear in masculine form, as in the many painted and carved images at China's Dunhuang and Lung-men cave temples and grottoes. In the Hall of 1001 Buddhas in Kyoto (the *Sanjusangendo*), Japan, stand 1,000 life-size androgynous-masculine gilded Kannons, each with a uniquely individual face—like snowflakes, no two alike. At the center of the orderly rows of 1,000 standing Kannons, sits a 1,000-armed, 12-foot-high *seated* Kannon.

Among the Bodhisattva's many various forms, the one with a 1,000 arms is considered the most sacred. Known in Japan as "Senju

Kannon," he or she has 11 heads topped with a Buddha head, able to look in all directions, and 1,000 arms with an open wisdom-eye in the palm of each hand. The many arms hold ropes, tridents, staffs, bows, arrows, spears, medicine, bells, teacups, swords, lotuses, rosaries, flowers, brushes, cushions, bowls—things the Bodhisattva can skillfully use to stop, convert, tie up, or cut down egotism, as well as to heal and nurture suffering beings. It is a dynamic image of active compassion bursting skillfully forth, while at the same time remaining centered and at peace. When you look at such a figure you think "Yes. This must be what selfless, skillful, limitless compassion *feels* like." We have several 1,000-armed Bodhisattvas of Compassion at Endless Path Zendo, several standing Kannons, a scroll of the bodhisattva seated by a stream, and a Tibetan thangka of a four-armed Avalokitesvara. All are reminders of, and encouragements toward, the realization of our own compassionate nature.

In 2006, Rose and I accompanied members of the Vermont Zen Center, Toronto Zen Centre, and Casa Zen (Costa Rica) to China where we visited noted Zen sites, among them Lin-chi's (J. Rinzai) monastery, where I was surprised to see a huge, maybe 20-foot-high, thousand-armed Avalokitesvara painted in blues, reds, golds—almost Tibetan style—standing behind the place where Lin-chi would have given his take-no-prisoner teishos. We were told that the image was a reproduction of the original, destroyed in the Cultural Revolution. It revealed what no books had hinted: Lin-chi's ferocious Zen was itself the expression of deepest love and compassion. "This is your Truth," he was saying. "As it is mine and everyone's. You *can* do it! You can awake! Don't dawdle!" Compassion is not simply sentiment or empathy. It is skillful action. Compassion is wisdom, wisdom compassion, hence the open eyes in each of those 1,000 hands.

According to *The Surangama Sutra*, the bodhisattva Avalokitesvara, a man living in the Buddha's time, became fully enlightened by dedicating himself to the practice of attention to hearing. Aitken Roshi told me that the essence of the Buddha's teaching lies in this inquiry, "Who is hearing?" a practice that takes you to the root of it all. Avalokitesvara, "Hearer of the Cries of the World," became the female Kwan-yin in China, Kannon, Kanzeon also Kanjizai—"The Lord who Observes All"—in Japan, the male Chenresigs in Tibet, and the source of Tara, "The Savioress," who emerged from a tear shed by the Bodhisattva upon seeing the extent of our world's sorrows. She is the Bodhisattva Avalokitesvara's most compassionate and most feminine essence.

There are times when our world's sorrows will overwhelm and stun us. And there are times when we will be deeply distressed by our own pettiness and self-centeredness. At such times we may try to convince ourselves that Zen is too demanding, that it is too difficult, and that it is beyond the likes of us. It is not a new problem, nor one we face alone. Keizan Jokin, one of Dogen's heirs in 13th century Japan, wrote:

> You may think, "The Way of the Buddha patriarchs distinguishes individuals and capacities. We are not up to it." ... Who among the ancients was not a body born of a mother and father? Who did not have feelings of love and affection, or thoughts of fame and fortune? However, once they practiced [Zen], they practiced thoroughly [thereby achieving enlightenment].
>
> Keizan Jokin, case 3, *Denkoroku, Transmission of the Light*, Francis Cook, trans.

How do we know but that in trying and failing and trying again, we are not setting in motion the very things we will most need to accomplish our goals? As a teenager I spent many hours shooting arrows at a target. At some point I seemed to realize that my many misses were all necessary steps toward eventually hitting the bullseye. If we persist in our

Zen practice, fears of coming up short, of not being smart enough, or strong or successful enough, get stripped away. In time we simply do our best and give our all, regardless of outcomes. To learn to live like this is, itself, worth a great deal.

The actual Zen practice of enlightenment won't open to us because of our looks, or our eloquence, or our smarts. It doesn't deal in such currency, couldn't care less who we know or what our salary or social standing might be. It's an iron mountain or, as Western fairy tales might put it, a glass hill. We try to scale it and, inevitably, we fall back down. Then we try again. Through trying and failing and trying again, our practice becomes genuine, and we ourselves authentic. This is how we mature. In this, too, we are not alone. Avalokitesvara, Bodhisattva of Great Compassion, matured in this very same way. Here's the legend of how, through bitter failure, his Vow matured and he gained 1,000 helping hands:

> The Bodhisattva Avalokitesvara, Bodhisattva of Compassion, "Hearer of the Cries of the World," looked down into the hells and saw them filled with suffering beings. "I will liberate all the beings in the lower realms," he vowed.
>
> Through countless ages he labored, descending into hell after hell, emptying hell after hell. After eons of heroic exertion, the Bodhisattva stood up and wiped the diamonds of sweat from his brow. He looked down into the now empty silent hells, and smiled. It was done. The hells had been emptied.
>
> Here and there a curling wisp of smoke rose. Now and then, in some vast cavern below, faint echoes sounded as a loose brick toppled from a pile of rubble. But the raging fires had been quenched and the great iron cauldrons of boiling blood were quiet. Sweet silence flowed through the dark halls. Even the raging demons were gone; the

horse-headed, the tiger-headed, the horned and fanged ones. They, too, in the end, had been released by the mighty efforts of the Compassionate One.

Suddenly there came a wailing scream and then, another. Flames leapt, smoke whirled, blood-filled cauldrons once again bubbled madly. Whips cracked, chains clanged, demons roared. The radiant smile faded from the Bodhisattva's face. In less than an instant all was exactly as before. The hells were again completely filled.

The heart of the Bodhisattva Avalokitesvara filled with sorrow. His head broke into eleven heads. His arms shattered into a thousand arms with an open eye of wisdom in each palm. With his eleven heads the Bodhisattva could now look in every direction to see the sufferings of every being. With one thousand wisdom-guided arms he could now reach into any realm to save those in need. Rolling up his one thousand sleeves, the Bodhisattva once again got to work.

Adapted from "The Legend of Avalokitesvara" in
The Hungry Tigress: Completely Revised and
Expanded Edition, Rafe Martin.

To gain insight quickly is not necessarily good. To take a long-ish time is not necessarily bad. Sometimes what is quickly won is never deeply felt. Quick successes may fade without ever developing in us the inner strength that persistence brings. When Britain stood alone against the rising Nazi tide, Winston Churchill stood in Parliament and announced, "Success is not final. Failure is not fatal. It is the courage to continue that counts."

It is the courage to continue that counts. What is courage but compassion in action? Persist, and you may find that you already have 11 heads and 1,000 hands. But even so, a challenge yet remains. How will you use them?

6

Hands and Eyes of the Bodhisattva of Great Compassion

With case 89 of *The Blue Cliff Record*—"Hands and Eyes of the Bodhisattva of Great Compassion"—two old Zen worthies explore the nature and activity of the 1,000-armed Avalokitesvara, by checking each other on how the Bodhisattva uses all those many hands and eyes. The case is as follows.

> Yun Yen (J. Ungan) asked Tao Wu (J. Dogo), "How does the Bodhisattva of Great Compassion use all those many hands and eyes?"
> Tao Wu answered, "It's like a man in the middle of the night reaching (groping) behind his head for his pillow."
> Yun Yen said, "I understand."
> Tao Wu said, "How do you understand it?"
> Yun Yen said, "The whole body is hands and eyes."
> Tao Wu said, "That is very well expressed, but it is only eight-tenths of the answer."
> Yun Yen said, "How would you say it, Elder Brother?"
> Tao Wu said, "Throughout the body are hands and eyes."

How *does* the Bodhisattva of Compassion use all those hands and eyes? Isn't Zen about being present for *this* cloud, *this* person, *this* rrrinng of the phone? How could multi-tasking be Zen?

Compassionate activity is the great Bodhisattva's entire being. Acting without a single self-centered thought for the sake of all is, for her,

[77]

second nature. Or first nature. But how does the Bodhisattva's Great Vow function? She has 22 eyes in 11 heads, plus an eye in every palm of 1,000 hands. How can she use all those eyes without confusion? How respond to all that those eyes simultaneously see? Which arm should she use, which hand extend? Emails are coming daily requesting the Bodhisattva to sign this petition, attend this rally, donate to this or that campaign. How not to end up paralyzed by so many choices, when in the thousand arms are not just pillows, but ropes, hatchets, steering wheels, computers, iPads, cell phones, swords, pens, life preservers, tea pots, and medicines? How can the Bodhisattva skillfully fulfill so many possibilities?

Kindness can be separative: *I* will help *you*. Compassion is intimate: "I *am* you." One is simile, the other metaphor. And because if I am you and the *I* (of me, myself, and I) is not there, it can't be a big deal, perhaps only something we notice after the fact. "What? I did that?" we may think. For example: I was once motorcycling on an empty country road when a deer leapt directly in front of me. Without thought, my hand grabbed the front brake and my foot stomped the rear one. Then my hand released the brake lever and rolled on throttle, keeping me upright despite the sudden stop, as picking up speed, I rode on having missed the deer by fractions of an inch. It all happened so fast, there was no time for even a thought of danger to arise. With no thought, there was no fear; with no fear, no adrenalin, and so my heart never sped up. My hand acted—and it was done. That swift life-saving response gave me a glimpse of something. What might it be like to live like that?

As Zen practitioners we have daily opportunities to interact and extend or lend (not impose) a hand, opportunities to integrate what we realize in the practice of Zen into our actual lives. Now. Just as we are. Lay practice especially keeps it real. Without such challenges Zen can become a high-class game: How many koans have we passed? How long have we sat? How many sesshin have we attended? But for what? In lay practice there's no evading, no putting it off. How *does* the Bodhisattva use all those hands and eyes?

Well, how do we raise a hand, taste a peach, think a thought, search a memory, catch a ball, grab a brake lever? How do we cry when sad and laugh when happy? We *are* a hand reaching for a pillow in the night. The eye sees, but does not see itself. The ear hears, but does not hear itself. This is our life. A soccer ball rolls toward the street. We put out our foot and stop it. Someone in line at the Post Office drops their wallet. We pick it up and hand it back.

Yet how many times might we balk, thinking, "I'll do it next time." Or ... fill in the blank yourself. How easy it is to separate hands and eyes, eyes and hands. Returning to this breath, the count of this breath—1, 2, 3—this unique koan point, eyes open and hands reach—for pens, brushes, ropes, pots, pans, cell phones, petitions, diapers, incense, sitting cushions. Is reaching back for a pillow in the night different than tying a child's shoelace, driving to work, buying groceries, answering the phone? Practicing this breath, this count, this koan, the world, in all its endless and specific variety, steps in. An old teacher once asked his attendant, "What is that sound outside?" It was raining and the attendant dutifully answered, "The sound of raindrops." The teacher was hardly convinced. How would you convince him?

How do we express intimacy *as* life? The great Chao-chou, (Joshu) when asked, "Why did Bodhidharma come from the West?"—a classic Zen way of asking about the highest teaching of Buddhism—answered, "The oak tree in the front garden." This had nothing to do with being illogical, or with stopping conceptual thought. I have heard such views and they miss the point. Nor was it a way of saying that Bodhidharma, who in another koan is identified as the Bodhisattva Avalokitesvara, was so compassionate that he made the then terribly difficult journey from Southern India to China for the sake of even this oak tree. Or, perhaps more to the point, that all beings—even this very tree—are

Buddha. Zen tradition is quite clear and it accepts none of those. Chao-chou was *intimate*. But would his answer, "The oak tree in the front garden," have been enough to convince the teacher who'd asked about that sound outside? What might Chao-chou have done to confirm it? How do you see it?

Attending to each breath, to each count of each breath; committing fully to the koan, fully *being* our practice, allows us to shift attention from an habitual, unconscious focus on the compulsively self-centered self, and change channels. When we do, a thousand eyes open: our eyes, birds' eyes, bugs' eyes, the eyes of rivers, mountains, trees, and clouds. Attending to the count, the breath, the koan, a thousand hands flex and reach. We discover that we don't need to glue all those arms on one-by-one, like so many merit badges. Instead, we find the one thousand arms that were always ours.

In the "Genjokoan" (Actualizing the Fundamental Point,") section of the *Shobogenzo: Eye of the Treasury of the True Dharma*, Zen Master Dogen lays it out clearly. "To study the Buddha Way is to study the self. To study the self is to forget the self. To forget the self is to be actualized by the myriad things. When actualized by the myriad things, one's own body and mind as well as the bodies and minds of others drop away. No trace of enlightenment remains, and this no-trace continues endlessly."

To forget the self doesn't mean to suppress or ignore it. Zen practice asks us to explore our deepest assumptions of what and who and where we are, to look deeply into such questions as "What is this self? Where is this self?" If we keep at it, we will see that our sorrow is that by believing ourselves to be separate and alone, we short-change ourselves, creating an isolation that not only harms us, but everyone and everything. This primal self-centered error in how we use our minds underlies our self-destructive behaviors and keeps us from living in harmony with all other living things. Real intimacy, which means living without a dualistic wall standing between us and everything and everyone else, is not something to simply be wished for, but is, as ongoing Zen practice can *confirm*, our real condition, our birthright.

The first vow of all bodhisattvas is to save living beings from the sufferings caused by the fundamental delusion of dualistic self-centeredness, of me "in here" and everyone and everything else "out there." Saving, in Zen, does not mean knocking on doors or handing out leaflets. An introductory or preliminary koan, one we work on after an initial koan like Mu or Sound of a Single Hand, but before beginning the formal books of koans such as *Gateless Barrier* or *Blue Cliff Record*, challenges us to "save a ghost." The path of the bodhisattva begins right now, right where we are. How shall we meet this challenge?

How *does* saving or freeing take place? And how does the Bodhisattva of Great Compassion manage it? How does she use—know *how* to use—all those hands and eyes? Forgetting the self also means that we no longer unconsciously project our own self-centered needs *onto* others, freeing them from us and from our own unconscious demands. Freeing ourselves by forgetting ourselves, forgetting our own self-centeredness, then, frees others and ultimately frees all. This sounds suspiciously narcissistic and overblown but it really comes down to simple things—counting this breath, *one, two, three;* experiencing this breath; questioning completely, "Who is hearing?" or becoming absorbed in a single koan point. By practicing sincerely, with focus and attention, forgetting the self in the count, the breath, the koan, the world steps in, not abstractly but uniquely and fully. Or rather, this very worm crawling on the wet sidewalk, this falling yellow leaf, this bright morning star, this raucous "*Caw!*" of the crow all step in, and because they do, we step out of our old sad dream of isolation and can begin to live in a truer world. The Vow is mutual.

Or if you want, don't forget the self. Hold onto it as tightly as you can. Really see if it is as solid and permanent as you think. Try to find it. Search and search. What do you find? Birdsong? Pain in knees, itchy nose, endless thoughts, feelings, sensations; sounds, sights, tastes, touch, smells? Is there anything more? Is there nothing more? Where is the self, my self? Is hands and eyes all there is? And how does the Bodhisattva use them? Master Dogen turned that around and asked, "How do hands and eyes use all those bodhisattvas?"

When Yun Yen said, "I understand," or, "I get it," was he saying, "Sure, I understand"? Or was he saying, "Aha! *Now* I get it!" But what is there to get? If, as the Buddha proclaimed upon his great enlightenment, we are already whole and complete, actually Buddhas from the start, how much more whole and complete can we become? Yet if we are already so whole and complete, indeed, Awakened, Enlightened, why don't we know it, why do we suffer so and cause such harm, and why must we work so hard to wake to what we already have, already are? Such questions gave young Dogen no peace. Yet, in time, that "no peace," opened his way to Great Peace, indeed.

What is the relation of seeing to doing, insight to action, silent and still zazen to our complex and demanding lives? Is it our aim to simply be calm and quiet? Or is that just the beginning of being able to do ... what, exactly? Mere forceful suppression of our own inner noise can't be more than a temporary solution. "It's like reaching back for a pillow in the night," says Tao Wu. Well, that certainly sounds easy enough, doesn't it? But is it? And what is this "night?" What is the darkness? Is it a simple antithesis of daylight? Is "night" a bad thing? And doesn't real seeing and doing demand full attention, full presence? Isn't that what Zen asks of us? So, how can a sleepy, half-awake, half-asleep condition, neither one nor the other, be of any real use?

Further, what about the two answers given by the teachers in the koan case? One says, "The whole body is hands and eyes," and the other "Throughout the body is hands and eyes." (Another translation says, "The outside is hands, in the inside is eyes.") Why two answers? Is one answer better? Is that why the case ends with the second response, as if it's, "Aha. Now that clinches it" ? Is there an actual point being made with these two answers and, if so, what is it? Or are these old teachers simply nit-picking and being clever? And if that's all that's going on, why should we even care about it? What relevance can such pedantry have? Is something real going on here or not?

And what about those eight-tenths? Is 80% good enough? What about a full 100%? Is this another one of those Zen *failures*, or is one teacher simply not willing to accord a full measure to the other, like the college professor who, on principle, won't give any paper, no matter how good, an A+? Zen master Dogen, in commenting on this koan, said that if real criticism had been implied, Tao Wu wouldn't have said— "You answer well. But it's eight-tenths." Instead, he'd have just said, "That's eight-tenths." Or "That's 80%." Why? What's Dogen getting at? Or is he, too, just being clever?

If we're not lost in our heads, going over the ache of unhealed wounds, planning for better future repartees, working on self-oriented schemes, then, when our friend slips, our hand reaches out to steady her; if a ball is overthrown we catch it and toss it back. Without a single intervening thought, with no "Should I?" or "Shouldn't I?" Nothing special at all. When the phone rings we pick it up and say, "Hello?" When the alarm rings we get up. This is life, the so-called "point" of practice. Living with less habitual, unconscious self-centeredness, we become more *present*. Being less here, we are, paradoxically more fully here than ever, and so can more clearly see and more appropriately act or not act, as the situation calls for.

A bodhisattva's "Great Vows for All" mature in the complex, imperfect mix of ordinary life. Yamada Roshi says that the point of practice is the maturing of character, which doesn't happen by willing ourselves into more mature versions of ourselves. It happens by losing ourselves, that is, losing sight of the self-consciousness that stands like a veil (or wall) between us and ... everything, even people we hold very dear. Dropping the whole self-centered deal by focusing so fully on this moment of practice that the very *concept* of an isolated, interior self fades or falls away, we touch base with the essential nature of all natures, human and non-human, the no-nature which is the key to our own missing humanity. But it is not a straightforward path marked by success after success. "Seven times down, eight times up; such is life" is how a Japanese folk saying puts it.

The practice of climbing to the top of the mountain of Zen, we're told, isn't really all *that* difficult. You work at it, keep at it, and in time— *Something*. But then, when you start back down the mountain, is when it hits you—*descending* is endless.

"How does the Bodhisattva use all those hands and eyes?" Stay with the practice, stay with the breath, stay with the koan. "Ripeness" as Shakespeare says, "is all."

7

Maitreya Bodhisattva and the Dream Within a Dream: Yang-shan's Sermon from the Third Seat

(An earlier version of this chapter appeared in *Before Buddha Was Buddha: Learning From the Jataka Tales*, Rafe Martin, Wisdom Publications 2017.)

Case 25, of *The Gateless Barrier*, "Yang-shan's Sermon from the Third Seat," goes as follows:

> Yang-shan dreamed he went to Maitreya's realm and was led to the third seat. A senior monk struck the stand with a gavel and announced, "Today the monk in the third seat will preach."
> Yang-shan rose, struck the stand with the gavel, and said, "The Dharma of the Mahayana is beyond the Four Propositions and transcends the Hundred Negations. Listen, listen."

Buddhist tradition says that Maitreya ("Gently Loving One"), the Future Buddha, is now a bodhisattva living in the Tushita Heavens. He's hard at work up there, developing the skillful means (upaya) he'll need to free suffering beings once he's back down here on Earth as a fully realized Buddha. "Skillful means" is one of the ten paramitas or "perfections" that bodhisattvas bring to completion on their way to Buddhahood. Generosity, morality, patience, vigor, meditation, inner strength, determination, wisdom, and knowledge are the others.

Iconographically, Maitreya Bodhisattva's posture is unusual. Instead of sitting in the traditional lotus or half-lotus posture, he sits in a chair, one knee crossed over the other, the index finger of his right hand at his cheek. His pose indicates that he is fully engaged in thinking up ways to save us all, and is just about ready to stand up and put his good ideas to work, too. However as time works differently in higher realms, "getting ready" can still mean a long time here on Earth. Galactic time is measured by the multi-million-year rotation of a galaxy, not the daily spinning of a planet. So a few hours of heavenly time could mean many thousands of Earthly years or even more. In fact, according to Buddhist tradition, Maitreya Bodhisattva's arrival, measured on Earthly clocks, rounds out to some five billion or so of our years. Shakyamuni Buddha is long gone and Maitreya Bodhisattva a long time coming. In this great gap of time it's up to each of us to keep the Dharma Wheel rolling, something which is taken seriously in Zen tradition. Here is a letter that the iconoclastic Japanese Zen master, Bassui, (1327–1387) wrote to a monk in response to an urgent request for guidance. Bassui was clearly deeply moved by both this gap in time between buddhas, and also by belief in the mappo, or Dharma-ending Age. In the letter he uses the name "Miroku" for "Maitreya," which would be traditional in Japan.

To a Monk in Shobo Hermitage
(At His Urgent Request)

In my boyhood this question perplexed me: Aside from this physical body, what replies, "I am so-and-so," when asked, "Who are you?" This perplexity having once arisen, it became deeper year by year, resulting in my desire to become a monk. Then I made this solemn vow: Now that I have determined to be a monk, I cannot search for truth for my own sake. Even after winning the supreme Truth I will defer Buddhahood until I have saved every sentient being. Furthermore, until this perplexity has been dissolved I will not study Buddhism or learn the rituals and practices of a monk. So long as I live in the human world I will stay nowhere except with great Zen masters, and in the mountains. After I entered a monastery my perplexity increased. At the same time a strong resolve arose from the bottom of my heart and I thought: Shakyamuni Buddha has passed already and Miroku, the future Buddha, has not yet appeared. During this period when authentic Buddhism has declined to the point where it is about to expire, may my desire for Self-realization be strong enough to save all sentient beings in this Buddha-less world. Even should I suffer the pangs of everlasting hell as a result of this sin of attachment [to saving], so long as I can shoulder the sufferings of sentient beings, I will never become discouraged or forsake this eternal vow. Furthermore, in practicing Zen I will not idle away my time thinking of life and death or waste even a minute in trifling good works. Nor will I blind others to the truth by trying to minister to them so long as my own [spiritual] strength is insufficient to lead them to Self-realization. These resolutions became part and parcel of my thinking, bothering me to some extent in my zazen. But I could not do otherwise. I constantly prayed to Buddhas for strength to carry out these resolutions, which I made the standard of my conduct in both favorable and unfavorable circumstances, under the watchful but friendly eyes of heavenly beings. Thus it has been up to the present. It is really pointless to tell you about these delusive states of mine, but as you make bold to ask I write here of my aspirations as a novice.

(Kapleau, *The Three Pillars of Zen*)

But, given Maitreya Bodhisattva's immense lovingkindness, Zen tradition adds that even he can't just wait billions of Earthly years. In fact, Zen insists that he's already here, wandering our Earth in the form of the pot-bellied, smiling, shaven-headed, big-eared monk, Hotei (Pu-tai or Budai in Chinese). With a sack slung over his shoulder filled with gifts that he freely gives away, and sometimes carrying a wine-gourd to share a toast with those who need a lift, he's no stickler for purity, but always ready with a smile, a helping hand, a timely word, a laugh, a cup of wine or tea, sweet buns, or toasted rice cakes. Until Maitreya arrives in all his majesty, Hotei will continue to walk humbly among us, skillfully and unobtrusively doing all he can to keep things on track. It's a tough job, perhaps especially these days. But in the tenth and final Zen Ox-Herding picture, we find him revealed as our own realized Nature. The encouraging verse to that picture goes:

> Bare-chested, barefooted he comes into the marketplace,
> Muddied and dust-covered, how broadly he grins!
> Without recourse to mystic powers,
> withered trees he swiftly brings to bloom.

We're all withered trees. But when Hotei shows up it's suddenly spring, and even the poorest little bush will begin to bud and put forth new leaves. Hotei has no need for self-conscious formulas or mystic powers; he's not a wizard. The selfless joy emanating from him does the job. The Irish poet, Seamus Heaney, wrote about a blind neighbor he knew as a child. "Being with her" he wrote, "Was intimate and helpful, like a cure/ You didn't notice happening" ("The Wellhead"). A haiku by Boncho reminds us of such silent, natural power:

> The brushwood,
> Though cut for fuel,
> Is beginning to bud.

Someone attentive and present, not caught up in the tangled loops of their own self-concern and self-interest, can naturally affect others.

At the entrance to many of the Zen sites we visited in China, were huge guardian figures meant to protect the temple from the unworthy. But when you walked past them and looked back, what you saw was a large, smiling Hotei beaming at you. At Endless Path Zendo, a wooden Japanese carving of Hotei greets you at the top of the stairs where you enter the zendo, and sees you out as you head back downstairs to the dokusan line. You may also see Hotei in your local Chinese restaurant where he's the "Happy Buddha" on the shelf above the cash register, a little populist image of something quite mysterious and profound. A poem by the Japanese Soto Zen master, Gesshū Sōko, (1618 –1696) says, "In heaven there is Maitreya,/on earth, Hotei-.../are they the same or different?" In pre-communist Tibet, large images of Maitreya were carved and painted into cliff walls, accompanied by the imploring words, "Come, Maitreya, come!" Similar images, as well as murals of Maitreya, adorn the more than 500 painted cave temples of Dunhuang, China, testament to 1,000 years (4th to 14th century) of devotion and yearning.

So ... about 1,200 years ago, Yang-shan, who was known to contemporaries as "Little Shakya," meaning a little *Shakyamuni* Buddha—high praise, indeed!—dreamt he was with Maitreya Bodhisattva in his heavenly palace. Not only was he included in that lofty company, but he'd been set in a seat of honor. In the first seat sat the historic Buddha Shakyamuni. Next to him was Maitreya Bodhisattva, the Future Buddha. And in the honored third seat, was Yang-shan himself.

What does this dream portend? Does it reveal that our "Little Shakya," suffered from an inflated ego; that he was a narcissist? Dreams, as we know and as Freud confirmed, can reveal a great deal, showing things we'd rather not admit even to ourselves, at least not to our waking, daylight selves.

Buddhist tradition says that there are countless worlds, heavens and hells in our universe; billions of galaxies, as many as the sands of the Ganges River is how old texts put it, each comprised of billions of stars, each sun with its planets, all drifting like snowflakes through a vast and endless night, and each galaxy or, perhaps, solar system, with its own realized, fully awakened Buddha. On some of those worlds,

Buddhas don't need strong words to teach as they do here where human beings can be so stubborn, rough-edged, and self-absorbed. On some of those more elegant worlds, the fragrance of incense, the taste of delicious food, even a sequence of notes forming some exquisite melody, may be all that's needed for the long-lived, happy beings who live there to reach enlightenment.

Lest you think, "Gosh. Why wasn't I born on one of *those* worlds?" there is a catch. Buddhist tradition says that our Earth is a "saha" world, "saha" being a Sanskrit word meaning "bearable" or "tolerable." Our world, then, is a Middle Earth set between the two great extremes of complete heaven and total hell. Which, it turns out, is to our benefit.

From the perspective of bodhisattvic aspiration, heavens themselves have a downside. Everything's so perfectly wonderful there, it's hard to establish any motivation to mature further. If every day is guaranteed to be great, why bother to do anything more than get out and enjoy it? On hell worlds it's the opposite. Things there are so relentlessly heavy, painful and dark, so loaded with "me, myself and I" locked in place by pain and fear, that even the thought of selfless practice—let alone the doing of it—would be impossible to sustain.

Fortunately on a saha world such as ours, this Middle Earth between heaven and hell, the difficulties and challenges combine to give us both motivation *and* opportunity to advance toward Awakening. Painful situations give us the motivation to ask the hard questions, and calm or wonderful moments of wholeness and joy tell us that life itself is a great gift, a mystery, and a happiness. On Earth things are not always so bad that we're always overwhelmed, nor always so good that we don't care to do anything but enjoy ourselves. Here we can actually walk the Path of the Bodhisattva, practice "forgetting the self," grow beyond habitual unconscious self-centeredness, and mature within, and through, and because of, our changing and challenging circumstances. Here we have both carrot and stick. Impermanence and injustice push at us so a need to know "Why? Why? WHY?" is never far from our minds. Here we also have access to teachings and practices that encourage and assure us that there is a Path that can help us resolve such questions as "Why was I born? Why must I die? Why do good people and innocent animals suffer, while selfish, cruel, and greedy folks prosper? Is this *really* all there is, and then we ... die?"

We should be grateful. It is our good karma, an expression of potential bodhisattvic intent to have been born on such a complex and beautiful planet. And, to be clear, our Earth, of course, has its own problems. Some may live here in virtual heavens, while many others are trapped in destructive and vicious hells. Injustice is woven into the condition of things here and many suffer terribly and unfairly. So it's not just other literal physical *worlds* out in space we're talking about. There are many worlds right here. Nonetheless, Buddhist tradition emphasizes that to be born on a saha world, a bearable world, (which may be interpreted as one of the realms here on Earth, a realm where pain and joy both exist) offers us the opportunity to proceed along the Path of the maturing bodhisattva and, to one degree or another, realize enlightenment.

And we're in luck, too. We're not alone. Maitreya is planning on joining us here soon. He's working hard, convinced that with enough skill, he might be able to do what's never yet been done by any previous bodhisattva or buddha—free *all* beings from suffering. Skill will be key. More than even 1,000 hands will be needed. Seated in a heaven, freed from temporal distractions, he's working on it right now, creatively coming up with idea after idea. Meanwhile, as Hotei, at the same time he's not abandoning our complex saha planet Earth, with its decidedly mixed bag of unfolding karma.

According to Aitken Roshi, when Yang-shan told his teacher, Kuei-Shan, about this dream, Kuei-Shan responded, "You have reached the level of sage." (So, no. He was not a narcissist.) Aitken Roshi adds that his own teacher, Yamada Roshi, said it's possible to be technically "enlightened" without being a sage. That is, someone can have a glimpse of realization, a shallow kensho, and not be transformed or particularly wise. Conversely, someone could be a sage, or worthy human being, without being enlightened in the technical sense of having glimpsed self-nature. So Kuei-Shan's saying, "You are an enlightened sage" is high praise.

Picture this in your own life: you are among a prestigious company, perhaps the greatest leaders in your field, and have been set in the honored seat. Facing you, row upon row, are the best of the best, with countless others tuning in via the Internet and TV. Suddenly it's announced that you are going to teach! Does this lofty heaven turn into sweaty-palm land? But Yang-shan doesn't falter. He stands up, strikes the gavel, *Whack!* and announces: "The Dharma of the Mahayana is beyond the Four Propositions and transcends the Hundred Negations. Listen, listen."

Why does master Wu-men, compiler of the *Gateless Barrier*, use the story of an old teacher's dream as a koan? Koans usually present the sayings and doings of noted teachers. But this is just a *dream* of teaching. What meaning can it possibly have? What's the value of a dream? What can words spoken in a dream do? And what does it mean to be "beyond" all phrases and "transcend" all philosophical positions? Is Yang-shan, in his dream, saying that while words and letters can point us toward truth, they can't reach it, or bring us to it? Is he saying that to know truth we must forgo words and move beyond anything written or spoken? Is that what he means?

Zen Master Dogen might disagree. In his view, words are as real and true as stars and cats, crows and clouds. A thousand years before Dogen, in *The Vimalakirti Sutra*—one of the few to focus not only *not* on the Buddha but on a layman, specifically the wealthy householder, Vimalakirti, a mythic figure contemporary with the Buddha, said to have attained the same level of realization as him—a goddess appears and talk with Shariputra, one of the Buddha's great disciples:

> The goddess said, "With your great wisdom, venerable sir, why do you remain silent?" Shariputra replied, "Emancipation cannot be spoken of in words. Therefore I do not know what I can say to you."
>
> The goddess said, "Words, writing, all are marks of emancipation. Why? Because emancipation is not internal, not external, and not in between. And words likewise are not internal, not external, and not in between. Therefore, Shariputra, you can speak of emancipation without putting words aside. Why? Because all things that exist are marks of emancipation."
>
> *The Vimalakirti Sutra*, Burton Watson, trans.

But what about values? How do they fit into "beyond *everything*?" In transcending everything do we leave values behind? Should we? If so, how would we fulfill our obligations to parents, family, nation, and planet? What kind of person would we then be? What *does* Yang-shan mean when he says that Truth lies *beyond* all philosophical positions, beyond yes, no, neither yes nor no, both yes and no and all their negations on through levels of consciousness and the three times of past, present, future, as well as beyond all words and phrases? Is he saying that the Dharma is a kind of spiritual blancmange, a bowl of pudding where "all is One"? What does "beyond everything" mean? And why did Wu-men think that a story of someone *dreaming* he said something about this would be helpful or significant? We don't want dreams, do we? Haven't we had enough of them? Don't we practice Zen because we want Truth? Isn't this why we sit, why we persevere? We want to wake up and grasp living truth, not linger in dreams. So what is Wu-men up to?

Then, again, what could be more *beyond* logic, reason, concepts, or positions than a dream within a dream? The old Celtic storytellers were masters of the narrative tool "interlacement." They'd start a story then have a character in that story tell a story, and then have someone in *that* story tell a story, and so on and on story within story within story like Russian nesting dolls, one inside the other, until our ability to follow what's a dream and what's real is gone. Then all we know, all we *can* know is what *is* this very moment. It alone is real. We are deep in a dream—perhaps deeper than ever—and yet, at the same time, more present than ever before.

In Zen, dreams and dream-like events are termed *makyo*, meaning mysterious, uncanny, strange, or delusive. Ultimately anything not perfect enlightenment is a makyo, a dream. From the perspective of deep practice-realization our ordinary waking life is itself a makyo or dream. Old songs tell the same tale: "Merely, merrily, merrily, merrily, life is but a dream." Edgar Allan Poe wrote, "All that we see or seem is but a dream in a dream."

There are low-level makyo when the mind becomes quiet and images, ideas, and sensations bubble up from unknown depths. After a few days of sesshin, complex and detailed movies can appear on the wall before us, or in the grain of the wood on the floor. Or the walls or floor might seem to ripple in waves. Such experiences are simply signs of deepening practice. We are encouraged by the old teachers to let them come—and go—like images in a dream and not to fixate on, or to get involved with them, but just to continue steadily on with our practice, counting each breath, experiencing the breath, sitting fully focused "thinking not-thinking," or absorbing ourselves in our koan.

Still, this dream of Yang-shan's is different. It feels mysterious, as if permeated with a kind of timeless, ungraspable meaning. When we wake from such a dream we might find the tang of incense on the air. "Was it real?" we may wonder. "Was it a dream?" Chuang tzu, the ancient Chinese philosopher sage, dreamt he was a butterfly. When he awoke he wondered: was he a man who'd dreamed he was a butterfly or was he a butterfly now dreaming he was a man? Which was real? And, how would he know?

Makyo can also carry deep significance. A voice in a dream might reveal a profound insight. A scientist might see the solution to a vexing problem, like Crick finding the spiral shape of DNA in a dream. A writer might come upon the solution to her novel-in-process, a musician hear the closing strains of a symphony they've yet to write. A Zen student could rise through layers of dream into awakening, all doubts fallen away. Artists, scientists, and religious practitioners have all known such possibilities. Creativity may depend upon it. We may call it vision or imagination, instinct or intuition, but there are clearly subtle realms like gifts, like grace. Maybe animals know it, too. After all, what *is* instinct?

Wu-men's commentary:

> Tell me, did Yang-shan preach or not? If you open your mouth you are lost. If you shut your mouth you will also miss 'it.' If you neither open your mouth nor keep it closed, you are one hundred and eight thousand miles off.

"One hundred and eight thousand" is a reference to the classical Buddhist understanding that with enlightenment, our 108 defilements become 108 perfections or virtues. Essentially, Wu-men won't let us off the hook. "If you say 'yes,' you miss it. If you say 'no,' you miss it. If you say neither 'yes' nor 'no' you miss it, too. What, then, is your move when even doing nothing misses the point? Wu-men puts this to each of us. How do we respond to his checkmate?

Can you say, "Yes, he preached," when he didn't actually say a thing? It was just a dream. (If you dream you wrote a novel, did you write it? Well, maybe you did in another world. Who knows?) But if you keep your mouth shut, indicating, "No, he didn't preach," Wu-men insists you've missed it, too. For something *did* happen. Yang-shan had a dream in which he preached words of truth. Those are facts. If you try to evade the dilemma by taking neither position you're also way off. Can you have a truthful life ignoring facts—things that actually happen? What kind of life would that be? Is there no right, no wrong, no up, down, hot, cold, good, bad? Does being "beyond all positions" mean anything goes? Try crossing the street when the light is red and see how that works out. Can willful ignorance be truth? Wu-men takes everything away: positive, negative, both, and neither (the four propositions) thereby echoing Yang-shan's words in his dream. What *does* it mean that the truth of the Mahayana is *beyond* every concept, every philosophical position? Was Yang-shan, our Little Shakyamuni, simply a rhetorician?

What is it to be awake? What is it to be asleep? What is a dream, and what is real? And how would we tell? Are we ourselves real right now, or like Chuang-tzu, are we dreaming still? Is it the one *or* the other? There are small, self-centered dreams that can plague us. "I dream of such and such and want it so badly I'll do anything to get it," is where fierce ambitions find their fuel. Less drastic versions abound and form the texture of ordinary reality: "*I'm* in here, *you're* out there. That's a tree. That's a raindrop. That's a cow." Ordinary reality is a kind of commonly agreed-upon dream. "We are such stuff as dreams are made on," says Prospero, magician and stage manager of *The Tempest*. There are also weird, mixed-up, rootless dreams, dreams of the night that are the result, as old Scrooge tells us in *A Christmas Carol*, of the undigested pudding we ate too late at night before going to bed.

And there are vast, noble dreams like the dream of Buddhist practice and bodhisattva vows, of wanting, indeed, of *vowing*, to save all suffering beings even while lost in dreams ourselves. This is the wild, crazy, magnificent dream that Zen would have us dream. This is Maitreya's dream right now. Not just becoming calm. Not just gaining a bit of peace. Not just being "in the zone," but the impossible dream without any stopping place, of entirely seeing through (not pushing away) all habitual self-centeredness and fully realizing Original Intimacy with stars, bugs, trash, wind, rain, clouds, mountains, rivers, people and liberating not only ourselves, but all things, living and non-living. A big dream, indeed.

Maitreya is working on making this real. He's not just thinking about it. He's putting in the time to bring it about. He's laying the groundwork. He means to do it. Out of vast empty-of-all-self-centered concerns and positions, solutions are coming. He's getting answers, seeing how it might be done. Compassionate ways are arising from his endlessly deep, endlessly evolving realization of Emptiness. He's turning his mind to it, putting his attention on skillful means. Maitreya, like Avalokitesvara and Samantabhadra, is in partnership with Manjushri, teacher of Buddhas, Bodhisattva of Wisdom. Through their collaboration he becomes not only the Gently Loving One, but the Skillful One as well.

Still, what's all the fuss about? Roshi Kapleau used to say that enlightenment is itself a dream. After all, it's the realization of our own Mind we're talking about; the vast and selfless Mind that's been ours from the very beginning. What are we going to get with enlightenment that we don't already have? The problem—and it's a big one—is that we don't yet know it. And because we don't know our own actual Mind, the miserable old beat we know all too well goes on and on. Suffering increases; the hells fill and refill. So this dream of enlightenment is an important dream, one on which a great deal of good depends. Without it, and without the efforts we make towards realizing it, we condemn even our own well-meaning selves to what are, at best, half-lives. We get up each morning and set off along what Zen calls the "mind road," hardly noticing the rising sun, the light on leaves at mid-day, the splendor of the moon and stars at night. We live in our thoughts about things, not things themselves. I cannot tell you how good this tea tastes. To know it you have to drink the tea yourself. Ordinary mysteries abound.

Yet, even while lost in the dream we live, we shouldn't discount the dream's value. Like Yang-shan's dream talk, there is truth in actions and words in a dream. "Life is but a dream," as the old song says. But the San, the Bushmen of the Kalahari, have a more intimate saying. They say, "There is a dream dreaming us." (*Heart of the Hunter*, Laurens van der Post.) Maitreya, Yang-shan, and Wu-men would approve.

For a dozen years or so, I had the good fortune to be invited to tell stories in Zuni Pueblo, one of the most traditional Native communities of North America. One day, as Rose and I were driving out of the pueblo, we saw a terrible figure striding down Highway 53, the road that runs through the pueblo. It was Atoshle, one of the fierce, punisher kachinas, or sacred beings, a kind of wrathful form of compassion such as you might find in Tibetan Buddhism. He wore a big, sacred, wooden mask with big sharp teeth and bulging eyes and long black, bloody hair—bloody because one hand held a bloody knife (made of painted wood)—and with that hand, Atoshle brushes back his bangs, leaving them blood-stained. He would soon pass Dowa Yalanne Elementary School, which looks out on Dowa Yalanne, Sacred Corn Mountain. Knowing that he was coming, the teachers would rush out to gather the children before he passed the school. If they didn't, and those children saw Atoshle, the punisher of wrongdoing, they would faint, dropping down onto the asphalt of the schoolyard.

Myth isn't just something in a book by Joseph Campbell. Myth is real. Atoshle is real. Roshi Kapleau had a Rinzai-like personality, forceful and direct, yet took quite a Soto-like stance, intuitive and sensitive, when it came to myth. He never spoke of "Buddha figures" or "Buddha statues." He always said, "The Buddha on the altar." Why? The Buddha is real. Maitreya is real. Yang-shan is real. So you and I are real, too. Dogen wrote in "Painting of a Rice Cake," in *Shobogenzo, Eye of the Treasury of the True Dharma*, "If you say a painting is not real, then the myriad things are not real."

Then again, how real is so-called "Reality"? Isn't it, in good part, what we imagine it to be, or what we are conditioned to believe it to be? Aren't we in large part what we are conditioned to believe ourselves to be? Ultraviolet photos of flowers, show them fantastically lit-up as if with neon landing strips to guide insects in towards the pollen. Human eyes don't see this. Dogen writes in the section "Mountains and Rivers Sutra" of his *Shobogenzo*, that fish and dragons see water like a palace, and if you told them that their palace was just water, they'd be shocked. Then again, we humans are shocked when we hear that mountains flow. We don't see it. Yet geologists and mountain climbers who find fossil seashells at the top of the Himalayas, confirm the truth that the highest mountains on Earth were once the bottoms of seas.

Is reality really "real," or is it, too, a kind of dream? "We *are* such stuff as dreams are made on." Bob Dylan in "Talking World War III Blues," adds, "I'll let you be in my dream if I can be in yours." Shibayama Roshi, in his commentary on this koan in *Zen Comments on the Mumonkan*, mentions that when the Japanese teacher, Takuan, was dying and was pressed by his disciples for a final verse, he picked up his brush and wrote one single word—*Dream*. Roshi Kapleau used to relate how, not long after he arrived at Hosshinji Monastery in Japan, a monk asked him, "Kapleau-san. Do you believe in dreams?" He told us that it took him many years of dedicated Zen practice before he'd grasped what that monk was actually getting at.

Do you believe in dreams? And who is that you that believes in dreams? What about this dream of Yang-shan's, in which a dream person teaches dream beings, in a dream palace, where a bodhisattva is dreaming up ways to save beings who are lost in dreams themselves—not to mention the dream being who wrote this talk, and the dream being now reading it.

Is it wrong that our life is a dream? Does that belittle or demean a thing? Do we need to change it? Do we need to make it more real? And what would that look like? How different would it be? Think again of what Yang-shan said in his dream within a dream, while he sat up in that lofty heaven with the Buddha and with Maitreya Bodhisattva: "The Dharma of the Mahayana *is beyond* the Four Propositions and *transcends* the Hundred Negations. Listen, listen." Isn't he saying that right now, not one day in the future when we finally "get it," but *right now*, Reality is itself beyond yes, no, up, down, dream, real, true, false, good, bad, wise, foolish? If so, then what is this Reality, and has Yang-shan expressed it fully? Is that 80%, or 100%, or what? And how about us? How will we express it? For every day we, too, are set in the honored seat and someone, some situation, some event puts a gavel in our hands and says, "Today you will teach. Now speak words of truth!" What do we do? Do we panic? Do we flub it? But "speak!" might mean the same as "live!" Or "show!"

When young Dogen arrived in China, seeking to advance further along the Way, he met an old monk, chief cook at a noted monastery some 85 miles away. The man had come to buy shiitake mushrooms from the Japanese travelers. (Dogen was still living on the boat at this time, as he had not yet been accepted for practice at any of China's monasteries.) Impressed by his conversation with the old head cook who was about to immediately head back to his distant monastery, Dogen asked him why he was not delegating this burdensome task of being head cook to others, so he could practice more thoroughly by sitting in formal zazen or by attending to koans. (Dogen also wanted the monk to stay longer so they might continue their Dharma talk.) The response he received affected Dogen deeply and would impact the rest of his life: "The reason for my being the chief cook at such an old age is that I regard this duty as the practice of the Way. How can I leave my practice to other persons?" When Dogen persisted in his questioning the old monk answered:

"You, a good man from a foreign country, perhaps do not understand what practice of the Way is, nor what words and letters are." Upon hearing this old man's remark, Dogen was "all of a sudden shocked and ashamed profoundly." Promising Dogen that he would discuss the matter some day in the future, he set off into the gathering dusk.

      Hee-Jin Kim, *Eihei Dogen: Mystical Realist*

When the gavel was suddenly put into this old man's hands he knew what to do. He stood up and spoke words of truth. The challenge is with each of us every day.

 Like "Little Shakya," and like the old head cook we must bring Maitreya's dream into the open and down to this Earth, so that even the brushwood cut for fuel and tossed onto the pile by the old wall, can start to bud. Wu-men knew what he was doing. He kindly took an old dream talk and, pasting it onto our foreheads like some miner's lamp, used it to help illumine our Way. In this way, too, Wu-men himself is a bodhisattva and the koan is not just a story in an old Buddhist book, any more than Atoshle is just a figure in a book on myth or native ethnography. The koan is real.

Wu-men's Verse:

In broad daylight under the blue sky,
He preached a dream in a dream.
Absurd! Absurd!
He deceived the entire assembly.

Yang-shan, having risen to Maitreya's lofty realm, had an incredible opportunity. Yet what he did there was rather ridiculous. Out in broad daylight, under the vast blue sky where nothing can be hidden and no dream long survive, he dared present a dream within in a dream. Wu-men says, "You've got to be kidding. Open your eyes, everyone. It's absurd!"

Wu-men, with his open Zen Eye, is calling out all our conceptual profundities as so much farce and even hodgepodge. All that big stuff, all those fine words trick us so easily. How about living a life right here on Earth, not up in some dreamy heaven, but eating when hungry, sleeping when tired, laughing when happy, seeing the sun rise in the morning and countless stars appear at night? What did we think Buddhism was about, anyway? After his great enlightenment, Lin-chi said, "There's not much to my teacher Huang-po's Buddhism, after all." What did he mean? Wu-men even says that Yang-shan tricked all those buddhas and bodhisattvas who'd gathered around Maitreya Bodhisattva, our Future Buddha. "What a joke," he says, "He tricked them all."

What "*them?*" *Us!* Yang-shan tricked us! And so did Wu-men, who's tricking us even now with this koan, and for that matter, with his whole *Gateless Barrier* koan collection. And here they are, both at it still, kindly and compassionately doing the work of Maitreya, tricking us out of our small, cramped, dreary, little, suffering-causing, alternatively self-doubting/self-asserting nightmares, putting us out in the bright sunlight where for a moment we can blink our eyes, and laugh and laugh. Hotei joins in. Maitreya sets down one leg, and gets ready to stand up.

For with this dream scenario those two skillful bodhisattvas, Yang-shan and Wu-men, have found a way to pull the wool *off*, not over, our eyes. Which is a pretty good trick wouldn't you say? Doesn't it make you want to break into a smile or even burst into laughter?

Unlike ordinary dreams of slumber, this koan's dream is an alarm clock ringing at our bedside, helping us to wake up and face the bright daylight of Right Now.

"Come, Maitreya, come!" Or is the great Bodhisattva already here?

8

The Bodhisattva Samantabhadra: A Buddhist Folktale

Fugen, the Japanese name for Samantabhadra, Bodhisattva of Compassionate Action, is usually depicted as sitting on a six-tusked elephant (one tusk for each of the six realms—god, human, warring spirit, animal, hungry ghost, hell-dweller). "He" (a linguistic designation only, as we shall see), presents fortitude in the compassionate acts that arise from selfless wisdom. So he, too, is a companion of Manjusri. Fugen's iconography may link him to ancient India and the god, Ganesha, the elephant-headed son of Shiva and Parvati, who moves forward with the strength of the elephant, or the cunning of the rat (his traditional ally/

vehicle). Whether by strength or by skill, Ganesha will break through, surmount, or circumvent all obstacles to enlightenment.

I know of no koans involving Samantabhadra. But there is a Japanese Buddhist folktale that reveals how this bodhisattva works his—or her—or their—wonders. My retelling of "The Legend of Fugen Bosatsu" is based on a version by Lafcadio Hearn, which he, in turn, based on one he found in an old Japanese storybook. This retelling originally appeared in an earlier book of mine, *The Hungry Tigress*. "Bosatsu" is the Japanese equivalent of the Sanskrit, "bodhisattva." So ...

About 300 years ago, in Japan, there lived a Buddhist Priest named Shoku Shonin. For many years, he had been a devotee of the Bodhisattva Samantabhadra, or Fugen, Bodhisattva of Compassionate Action. Day and night Shoku Shonin focused his mind on the Bodhisattva. Day and night, he recited verses from the sutras that promised Fugen's protection. Shoku Shonin had only one wish: to see Fugen.

One day, as Shoku walked through the streets of a local village, he overheard two merchants talking about a woman who lived in the town of Kanzaki, several days walk away. This beautiful woman, they said, attracted large crowds each evening by dancing while dressed as the Bodhisattva Fugen. Shoku was shocked, and he was outraged.

That night he had a dream. In the dream a voice spoke to him and said, "Go to Kanzaki and watch her dance." "Foolishness!" proclaimed Shoku upon awakening. "Devil's promptings will never move me." And he didn't go.

The next night, the same dream with its dream-voice came again. "Go to Kanzaki and watch her dance." "Never!" said Shoku.

The third night, the dream came again. "Watch her dance," insisted the voice. And that morning when Shoku awoke, he said to himself, "Perhaps I am called to end this sacrilege."

He tied on his straw sandals, set the wide, deep bowl of his monk's traveling hat upon his head and, ringed staff in hand, set off for Kanzaki. After several days of brisk walking he entered the town. It was early evening, the sky beginning to darken, a few stars faintly glittering overhead. But a crowd had gathered and torches were lit. Then, as the sky grew dark, as if by magic, the woman appeared on a small stage in the courtyard. Breathtakingly beautiful, she was dressed in the flowing, Indian-style robes and necklaces that, in paintings and sculptures, adorn the Bodhisattva Fugen. Keeping time with a small hand-drum she began to dance. Her jewels sparkled in the torchlight and all the men, except for the priest Shoku Shonin, entered into a trance of delight.

Shoku Shonin's rage grew. It was blasphemy. Yet, gradually, an inexplicable change overtook even him. He grew calm, and a deep peace spread through his limbs, rising from the soles of his feet up through the crown of his head. The night sky shimmered and the ground seemed to drop away beneath his feet. What did he care? The dance! The dance! Such joy radiated through the universe from this woman's dance. The stars were dancing, the earth was dancing. His eyes seemed to penetrate the darkness, and it seemed as if, out in the night, the trees, the animals in their holes, the people of the town were all moving, all breathing in time with, were all part of, this wonderful dance. Even the beating of his own heart, the rush of air in and out of his lungs, the ticking of his pulse, were part of the miracle of this perfect dance.

A slender ray of golden light shot from between the perfect, arched brows of the dancing woman. Dazzled, Shoku Shonin closed his eyes. When he opened them, there, before him on the little platform in the courtyard, he saw not the woman, but the radiant figure of the Bodhisattva Fugen seated on a great six-tusked white elephant, golden beams of light shooting all around.

Tears of joy trickled down Shoku Shonin's face. His life-long dream had been fulfilled. How long he stood there gazing, drinking in the scene before him, he never knew. When he came to himself at last, the stage was bare. The torches had burned low. The last of the men were leaving. Coins and favors littered the dancing platform.

Shoku turned away and stumbled along the street. As he left the village, he heard a faint tinkling, as of little silver bells. There before him stood the dancer in the robes of Fugen. "Tell no one," she said, "of what you alone have seen this night. Go in peace, old friend." And she was gone. A faint scent, like heavenly incense, lingered on the night air. Then it, too, was gone, blown away on the wind.

Dazed, Shoku started walking again. Several days later he discovered that he had arrived back at his own temple. Of his long walk home he remembered nothing.

Shoku told no one of his strange experience. But at last, years later, near death, he related the whole incident to a brother monk. His final words were, "Free, for compassion's sake, to take endless forms throughout the limitless universe, they do not despise the lowly and ignoble."

And putting his palms together Shoku Shonin peacefully died.

Section 2

THE Bodhisattva

Introduction

The Buddha as *The* Bodhisattva

Jataka tales are stories, purportedly told 2500 years ago by the Buddha himself, of his own past lives. It was one of his ways of teaching. Through these tales the Buddha resolved complex issues in his sangha by revealing root causes and by demonstrating the working of cause and effect, or karma, which does not begin—or end—with a single lifetime. In the jataka tales he also reveals his own personal path of maturing from ordinary, self-centered being to enlightened Buddha. Over time these tales became immensely popular in Buddhist Asia, and have remained a primary and populist way—through storytelling, theater, painting, and sculpture—of teaching bodhisattva values and Buddhist aspiration.

Around 400 CE, 547 such tales were collected together to form the Pali *Jataka*, which opens with a separate lengthy introductory story—the *Niddankantha*—dramatizing the Buddha's decision, as a sage long ago who meets with Dipankara, the Buddha of a past world age, to abandon personal salvation and become an awakened Buddha, able to benefit all. The stories in the Pali *Jataka* tend to emphasize karma or cause and effect, and while many reveal the compassionate mind of a bodhisattva, many are re-cyclings of older Indian animal fables and epic fairy tales put into Buddhist clothing. Additionally, 34 deeply influential and inspirational jatakas form a Sanskrit Mahayana text—the *Jatakamala* or *Rosary or Garland of Jatakas*. Composed by Aryasura around 400 CE, these tales emphasize the limitless compassion of *the* Bodhisattva, (the Buddha in past lives), and are clearly meant to inspire bodhisattvic aspiration and behavior. Additional jatakas are scattered throughout sutras and other Buddhist literature, though many were also lost as oral traditions faded over time. By the time the Pali and Sanskrit written collections were created, jatakas had already been canonical within Buddhist tradition for some 800 years, or within 100 years of the Buddha's death, or parinirvana.

Taken as a whole, jataka tradition has had a tremendous effect on the popular imagination of all Buddhist countries and traditions. Jatakas were a primary way of teaching Buddhist values, aspiration, and ethics. However, while noted Zen teachers, like Lin-chi and Hseuh-t'ou in China, and Dogen and Hakuin in Japan, make clear jataka references, Zen tradition itself has, on the whole, left jatakas pretty much untouched. Perhaps this is changing. Given Western traditions of animal fables, fairy tales, Aesop's tales, and such, jatakas may help give Zen practice a clear ethical foundation. Yeats wrote, "In dreams begin responsibilities." By rousing and moving the imagination, our real life, the one we aim to create, begins to come into being. As the precepts or ethical teachings are not taken up as koans and investigated personally until near the end of formal koan training, the jatakas can help align ethics with the path of practice from the start. As Zen in the West is primarily a lay movement, this is doubly important. Lay Zen practitioners are not isolated in monasteries, but must live their practice every day, out in a complex and challenging world. So having the jatakas as background to formal practice roots Zen in the ethics of compassion, making the Path of the Bodhisattva that much more clear.

While many jatakas offer models of noble character, there are some that are so self-sacrificing as to be disturbing. The opening tale of the *Jatakamala*, "The Tigress," is one of the most famous. In it the Buddha, as a sage long ago, offers his body as food to a starving tigress to keep her from devouring her own cubs. In jatakas in the Pali collection, the Bodhisattva slices bits from his arms and legs to feed vultures in a graveyard, and in another tale, gives a pigeon's weight of his own flesh to a hawk, to save the pigeon it has caught to eat. In such tales—there are others—compassion is itself "gone beyond," and the Bodhisattva becomes capable of essentially doing almost anything imaginable in order to personally save others from suffering; his Vow is that strong.

But despite, or perhaps because of their high ideals, the jatakas are not simply hagiographies. There are tales, too, that don't shy away from revealing the Buddha's personal struggles, even occasional stumblings and failures, along the Path. Such honesty is refreshing, and helps leaven some of the more cloying aspects of religious idealism. It is encouraging to see that, just like us, the Buddha had his issues, that he was not always radiant and perfect but, rather, a very human work in progress; a person who persevered.

In the next chapters, several jatakas with commentaries on them from a Zen perspective, will be our focus. It will be a way of extending our understanding of the Way of the Bodhisattva. One of the tales will be about a failure, and the others—all brief—will, to one degree or another, show deepening fulfillment of the great ideals of wisdom and compassion.

9

Why Be Born Human?
The Bodhisattva Makes a Mistake

(An earlier, less complete version of this chapter appeared in *Before Buddha Was Buddha: Learning From The Jataka Tales* by Rafe Martin.)

The Campeyya Jataka, #506 in the Pali collection of 547 such tales, goes essentially like this:

Long ago, when the Campa River was the boundary between the kingdoms of Anga and Magadha, there was fighting between the two realms. One day the King of Magadha, fleeing pursuing Anga warriors, came to the river boundary and thought, "Better to drown in the river than be slaughtered by foes," and spurring his horse forward, plunged into the water.

Down on the river bottom the naga-serpent king, Campeyya, was enjoying himself, listening to naga musicians play on instruments of ivory and gold and watching naga maidens dance. The river bottom had been strewn with gold and silver powders, and the flame-bright coral trees hung with diamonds, rubies, emeralds, and pearls. Suddenly, the music stopped and the maidens grew still. Looking up, the naga king saw a man on horseback drifting down through the water. He saw nobility on the man's face and, taking a liking to him, allowed horse and rider to arrive safely on the river bottom. Rising from his pearl throne, the naga king offered the stranger his own seat, saying "Fear nothing, friend. I have only your welfare in mind. Who are you and why have you entered my realm?"

Then the defeated king of Magadha opened his heart and poured out his troubles. The naga king said, "The solution is simple. You shall rule both Anga and Magadha."

For six days, the king of Magadha remained on the river bottom as the guest of Campeyya, the Naga King, but on the seventh, he rose from the river and, with the serpent king's protection over him, defeated the king of Anga. After that, he ruled both kingdoms, all warring ceased, and there was great friendship between the human king and his benefactor, the king of the nagas. To honor their friendship, the new king of the two kingdoms had a pavilion of gold and jewels built on the riverbank. There, each year, the glittering serpent king rose from the river and, surrounded by retainers, took human form to receive precious gifts from his friend, the human king.

At that time, the Bodhisattva (the Buddha Shakyamuni in a past life) was the eldest son of a very poor family. Awed by the riches he saw each year at that gift giving, he wished that one day he, too, might enjoy such a life. Not long after this, he died. The naga king, Campeyya, also died. Given his merit, the Bodhisattva's wish was fulfilled. He came into life as the new king of the nagas of the Campa River.

Looking down along his long serpentine body, the Bodhisattva thought, "What have I done? I have gained riches but have wandered from the true path. My aim is enlightenment. To achieve it I must be human." Though surrounded by riches, he felt not joy, but shame. But when the naga maiden, Sumana, exclaimed, "Has a god taken life among us? Such is the beauty of our new king!" and the naga musicians took up their instruments of crystal and pearl, and the naga maidens began to dance, the Bodhisattva set aside his sorrow and, taking human form, sat in splendor on his throne of pearl. Then, with Sumana as his wife, the Bodhisattva ruled his underwater realm.

One day he thought, "Though I dwell in splendor as a Serpent King, I am far from ultimate Truth. It is better to be human, even a human being without wealth or power. For even ordinary human beings can practice the Path of Liberation, the Way of the Bodhisattva. What I have gained is not the true freedom."

Then, in order to develop the virtue he would need to regain actual human life, the Bodhisattva fasted one day each week. Eventually, finding this too easy, he decided to return to the land once a month and there keep his vows of fasting and non-violence. When the half-moon appeared, he left the river. Taking the form of a silver cobra he coiled around an anthill and lay in the dust with lowered hood. Yet even in this form the people recognized him and did not strike or chase him. Instead they offered flowers and perfumes, and when he returned the following month, they built him a cloth pavilion where he could receive their offerings in comfort. In this way a pattern was set.

One day Sumana said to the Bodhisattva, "The world of men is filled with treachery. I want to know that you are safe when you are there." The Bodhisattva pointed to a clear pool in their garden beneath the river. "If someone hits me, this water will turn cloudy. If a winged garuda, enemy of nagas, carries me off, the pool will become dry. If a snake charmer captures me, the water will turn the color of blood." Embracing his wife, he left the river and returned to the anthill.

A Brahmin who'd just learned powerful spells in the city of Takkasila heard of this miraculous silver serpent and thought, "With my spells I might control this snake and become rich." Repeating his mantras, he approached the Great Being who lay coiled in his cobra form. When the Bodhisattva heard these spells, it felt as if fiery splinters and iron nails had been pounded into his head. His mouth burned and his eyes stung. Flicking out his tongue, he raised his head and spread his hood. But, seeing the snake charmer, he thought, "One drop of my poison could shatter his body. He does not know my power. But I have taken vows and will not harm him." And lowering his hood he lay back down.

Now feeling secure, the Brahmin chewed herbs and spit them on the great serpent's head, making a fiery blister arise there. He smeared his hands with more of the herbs, dragged the Bodhisattva from beneath his cloth canopy, stretched him out full-length on the ground, pinned his head with a forked stick, beat him with a club, and spit more herbs into his mouth, which filled with blood.

"Snake," he said. "You are in my power. Resist and it will be even worse for you." Pushing and folding the Bodhisattva's body, he shoved him into a basket, and set off for the next town. Once there he gathered a crowd and made the naga lord perform. And what a dance it was! The Great Being moved his body with such grace and speed he made circles, squares, and lotus flowers in the air; made one, ten, a hundred, a thousand hooded heads appear. The people loved it, and as they tossed jewels and coins, the Brahmin thought, "If this snake brings me such reward in even a small town, what might it do for me in a big city or at the royal court?" He bought a cart, put the naga king's basket on it, and drove toward the capital city of Benares. In towns along the way the serpent king danced and brought the Brahmin yet more wealth. But the Bodhisattva refused to eat. "If I eat the frogs he kills for me, he'll only kill more. I cannot allow it. I have taken vows." Offered fried cakes and honey he thought, "If I eat these delicacies I'll be stuck in this basket until I die," and, again, he would not eat.

Sumana was worried. Where was her husband? What had happened to him? She went to the pool beneath the river and found it the color of blood! A snake charmer had him! At once she set out to find him. Arriving at the anthill she saw signs of a struggle. Taking the form of a radiant goddess, she flew through the air. Alighting outside a village she heard talk of a serpent's dance and a snake charmer's journey to the capital. Weeping, she rose again and flew toward Benares, where preparations for a royal show were underway. The palace courtyard was strewn with white sand and a fine carpet set at its center. Then the Brahmin put his jeweled basket on the carpet, and charmed the Great Being forth. When the Bodhisattva danced he formed circles, squares,

The Bodhisattva Makes a Mistake

and lotus flowers, made ten, a hundred, a thousand hooded heads appear. Jewels and coins fell like rain.

Suddenly the Serpent King Bodhisattva stopped. Holding his body still, he gazed into the sky. The crowd, the Brahmin, and the king, all looked up, too—and were filled with wonder. For standing in the bright air was a beautiful shining woman, weeping. Tears fell from the Bodhisattva's eyes, too, and he crawled back into his basket where he lay hidden.

The king called to the woman in the air, "Are you a goddess? For not human is your power and shining beauty. Who are you and why do you weep? Is it for rage or sorrow?"

"I am no goddess," answered Sumana, "but a naga queen who weeps both for rage and sorrow. My lord's power, like that of Shakra, king of the gods, is so great his single breath might destroy your city. Yet such is his love of goodness, that he dances harmlessly before you. He has taken vows and will not strike. Though his body is bruised and blistered, his sides bony and thin, beneath the Campa River, sixteen thousand nagas call him king. This snake charmer has taken a great lord for his profit. As one desirous of merit will you not, great King, set him free?"

Then the king offered the Brahmin the finest bull of his herd, 100 of the best cows, 100 chests filled with gold and gems, and a golden throne shaped like a flax flower with blue silk cushions like petals. "Release this holy naga lord," he said, "and all this is yours."

"Willingly," said the Brahmin.

The Serpent King Bodhisattva came out of the basket and went into a flower. Shedding his serpent shape he then reappeared as a young man in robes of gold. There he stood, handsome as a god, and Sumana, descending from the skies, stood beside him. Those who had come thinking to simply see a serpent's dance found themselves well rewarded!

After the king and his nobles escorted the Bodhisattva and Sumana back to their river, before parting he asked if he might see their underwater palace. Then all of them entered the river together and descended to the river bottom. The human king and his court were astonished by the riches they saw. "Why, Great Being," he asked, "did you leave such magnificence to lie on an anthill in the dust?"

"All such treasure," said the Bodhisattva, "is nothing compared to the treasure of human birth through which enlightenment may be realized. Hills of pearl, groves of flame coral trees, clusters of jewel-fruit, diamonds, emeralds, rubies, sapphires, mountains of gold, lakes of silver—take what you want and use it for good." Filling chests with treasure, the human king and his court returned to their own realm. However, they'd been given so much gold that, as they travelled, the excess spilling from their treasure carts stained the earth. Which is why the ground from the shores of the Campa River to the ancient city of Benares remain the color of gold today.

Commentary

A Buddhist parable says that a blind turtle, swimming in an endless sea, rises to the surface once every 100 years and lifts its head from the water. A board with a hole in it floats randomly on that endless ocean. What are the odds that the blind turtle will put its head through the hole in the board? Those are the odds that Buddhist tradition says we have each faced and beaten in being born human; the odds of encountering the Dharma once we are human are said to be even longer. Perhaps a vow lies at the root of our success, a vow and a great deal of work. And, yet, how easy it is to take it all for granted: "Sure, I'm a human being but there are billions of us. So what? And, yes, I sit in zazen, but so do many others. Again, so what?"

Then again if, as the tale suggests, there's something more to human life, something valuable that's only made possible by our being human, then the story is a gift, a wake-up call and a warning: if we don't use the rare opportunity of this life, this treasure, how long might it be before the chance comes round again? The sea of time and space is endless; the turtle quite blind.

Tibetan Buddhism is clear on the effort it takes to attain human birth. Specific conditions must be met for egg and sperm to coalesce and work together to create a human being: pure essences of the parents; the five universal elements of earth, air, fire, water, and space; the three biological humors—phlegm, bile, and air; plus a fourth link beyond physical conditions, supplied by the parents, that is karmic and emotional, attracting the being to a particular set of parents. After this first begins the arduous work of forming a body and mind, traversing animal forms, and rising into a human condition from an initial curd-like mass at one with the mother. Pushed through the birth canal we take a first breath and then, at last, start the difficult process of individuation, in which we lose our original sense of connection and awareness of the thoughts and feelings of others. We solidify, imagine ourselves more and more alone and isolated, and start reacting as if that aloneness was itself totally real. After all that, if our karma ripens, we may begin spiritual practice, slowly finding our way back to our original sense of connection, without losing what our uniquely matured life has now made possible.

Why make this effort to become human and why, once human, strive to mature? From a Buddhist perspective the answer is our fundamental Vow, the vow of Mind (not intellect) to know itself, Awaken, and be of benefit to all; a bodhisattva vow, which expresses the fundamental, usually unconscious, aspiration of all living things. If in reality all living things are my own Self in various forms, why wouldn't I want to realize this and be of help? If my arm hurts don't I rub it? If my head hurts wouldn't I soothe it?

According to Buddhist tradition, it is only from a human condition that selfless awakening is possible. The vow to awaken propels us. But this is not a vow simply made in words. The flower vows to turn to the sun and open; the apple seed vows to become a tree producing apples; the caterpillar vows to free itself from the cocoon, grow wings, and fly. A Zen student's Great Vows for All, or Four Vows, are a conscious reminder of a fundamental determination to become what we truly are, and fulfill our potential.

While there are, and have been, billions of human beings on Earth, what does it mean to be fully *human*? Does having two legs, eyes, ears, nose, hands, brain, and feet, sum it up, automatically making us human beings? If so, then there are billions, indeed. Though even billions is not that many, not if we consider the billions of other planets in our galaxy which may be capable of life, and the countless billions of planets in billions of other galaxies. Then the billions of Earth humans may turn out to be a relatively small number. But if by "human being" we mean something else, specifically someone wise and compassionate, not driven by greed, anger, ignorance, or fear, someone who can be counted on when the going gets rough, then that number may be relatively small. (Though, oddly, when the chips are down, such people seem to show up as if they've been waiting in the wings all along.) What does it take to be or become such a genuinely human, human being?

Buddhism says that there are six realms—realms of gods, warring spirits, hungry ghosts, animals, hell dwellers, and human beings. These realms can be understood mythically, literally, psychologically—or all of these simultaneously. If we take it psychologically, then it's a way of recognizing that we may only be fully human for part of each day and only to varying degrees. When we're consumed by anger and seek to fight those who seem to oppose us, we are warring spirits, or asuras. When we're tormented by unfilled wants and desires, we're hungry ghosts, or pretas. When everything is going great and we float on air, we are gods, or devas. When passions and instincts drive us and life seems beyond control, we are animals. (Though such a view short-changes and demeans actual animals and their individual talents, graces, and wisdoms.)

The Bodhisattva Makes a Mistake

When we suffer terrible anguish and pain we are in hell. When we are truly human, what is it like, then?

The parable of the blind turtle gains power when we see it as a way of talking about becoming fully human, not simply as about having a human body and form. Becoming fully human is going to take effort, and involve many attempts, many steps along the way. Yet the difficulties—even the failures—are important. They are not just our hard luck. If we accept and work with them, they are what helps us mature, forcing us to grow beyond complacency. As human beings we recognize impermanence, and understand how little time we have to fulfill our Vow. With human consciousness we face unanswerable questions— Why are things as they are? Why is there injustice? Why do bad things happen to good people? Why is there greed, anger, and ignorance? Why environmental destruction, misogyny, homophobia, and racism? Why do I make so many mistakes though I mean to do otherwise? Why was I born? Why am I here? Why must I die?

The challenge of such questions can be hard to live with. Rather than making us wiser or more open and compassionate, they can also make us want to run and hide or simply lose ourselves in entertainment, news, shopping, hobbies, work, conspiracy theories, whatever takes the edge off. Certainly this is not necessarily all bad. Meaningful work, hobbies that use our talents or relieve our stress, time spent with family deepening our care and love, are valuable. They are part of our being human. Perhaps it depends on whether we're running from or towards. But as human beings we have choices—some good, others less so. This is "free will." But if we simply turn away from facing the difficulties and growing through them, the story of the Buddha's home-leaving can become a parody. Now a privileged prince leaves his sheltering palace and upon encountering the four ego-destroying signs (old age, sickness, death, and a path beyond that), turns around, runs back inside, pulls down the blinds, locks the door, and turns up the music, suppressing his own Great Vow. With the hero or heroine's Call refused, the summons to the Quest denied, myths world-wide say that our potential festers, and we ourselves become the monster Hold-Fast. Stuck in place, we can only stagnate, until a new hero/heroine comes along and sets us free. Joseph Campbell mapped this out clearly in his classic *Hero with A Thousand Faces*, a ground-breaking primer on the nature of myth. And yet, as the Campeyya Jataka makes clear, from a Buddhist perspective, despite its difficulties, ordinary human existence, just as it is, is *supremely* valuable. Why is this? Because as human beings we can realize Enlightenment.

In this jataka a more than human, nearly godlike condition of ease, pleasure, wealth, and power, is represented by the shimmering, treasure-filled, underwater realm of the nagas, a psychic zone that is fluid and rich, vibrant with beauty, sensuality, and wisdom. Inhabited by nagas, traditionally seen as non-human serpent beings with handsome male or beautiful female human heads and upper bodies, that taper down to a snake's tail. Sometimes they may have cobra hoods—one or several—above their human heads. They can also appear as cobras, or as giant cobras, or as many-headed cobras, or as human beings, though it's said that if you look closely at a naga appearing as a human, you may notice a glittering cobra hood-like aura surrounding it. Nagas can be sensual, as well as wise and spiritual. It is said that the Buddha, recognizing that human beings were not yet evolved enough to receive the complete Prajna Paramita (transcendental wisdom) teachings gave them to the nagas for safe keeping. Presenting them to anyone not mature enough would be like giving a loaded gun to a child. Maturity is important. Emptiness does not negate ethical behavior. Wisely, the Buddha gave these profound teachings in fullest form to the nagas. Hopefully, the nagas will still be around to pass them on to us, when we humans are finally grown up enough to use them wisely.

For, unlike dragons of Western tradition who hoard jewels and gold, nagas can be generous as well as have Dharma affinities. In the legendary life of the Buddha, the naga king, Kala Naga Raja, chanted ancient songs predicting the Buddha's enlightenment, and the naga king, Mucalinda, raised his cobra hood over the newly awakened Buddha to protect him from a violent storm. While snakes have been feared, even despised, in European traditions, throughout indigenous America serpent beings are, as in Asia, respected—a positive sign for the flourishing of Dharma in the Americas. And why not? Snakes live unseen, mysterious lives in the depths, seem to possess a cool and ancient wisdom, and though mere flesh and bone, can flow like water. What's more they can shed their skin, reappearing as if newborn. The double helix of entwined serpents, the ancient healer's sign, is familiar to South American shamans, and perhaps, not coincidentally, is also the shape of the serpentine DNA coiling at the core of every cell on Earth. In Kundalini yoga, the energy rising up the spine is a "serpent power." In Buddhist tradition, greatly enlightened beings who have recovered the mani (wish-granting) jewel from the depths, may, like the great Buddhist teacher Nagarjuna, be honored with the name of *nagas*.

Still, are actual wise naga beings a human fantasy, or do they have some basis in ordinary reality? Perhaps the intelligence, curiosity, friendliness, linguistic skills, and x-ray vision of whales and dolphins—land dwelling mammals who 50 *million years ago* returned to the sea, grew large, complex brains, and developed peaceful social systems—provide models for these serpent-like holders of highest wisdom. A professional diver and his camera crew snorkeling among sperm whales (which have the largest brains on the planet), soon after a sperm whale calf had been born, recounts:

> ... they were welcoming us to the most sacred of events—the birth of a new baby whale. They welcomed us, the same species from the same island as those who had killed them less than thirty years before. That is why I know they are

so much more intelligent, so much more sophisticated, so beyond us humans.

The epilogue to *Carnivore Minds* by G.A. Bradshaw, the source of that quote, concludes:

> Despite what humans have done, sperm whale culture remains inclusive, rooted in the belief of mutual respect. For sperm whales, [the largest predator on the planet] the counterpoint of victimhood, revenge is obviously unnecessary, and so it has failed to find a place within their society. Perhaps their seemingly infinite compassion comes from the vast oceans where they live. There space and time, subject and object, fuse in the sperm whale click-and-coda language that envelops the planet like an invisible connective tissue. It is in this gentle world that we find an ethical exemplar who should inspire our own species' evolution.

There is an awkward wrinkle to the lovely possibility that whales have some connection with the mythic nagas. We hope for many reasons that whaling will end, and soon. It is a barbaric practice and a cruel one. But additionally, if the Buddhist legend of the nagas has truth to it, then our own maturing as a species may depend on their being around, able to share teachings they hold in readiness for us, with us, once we're finally ready to receive them. May that day come soon!

Given all this, how could a human being struggling with poverty be better off than not just a naga, but a rich and respected naga lord? A lord among nagas would have wealth, wisdom, knowledge, long life, as well as access to beautiful naga maidens. Who hasn't wished for such a life? Who hasn't dreamed of a life of beauty, comfort, pleasure, wealth?

The Bodhisattva Makes a Mistake

This jataka provides the classically Buddhist response: "That's all good, it's true. But even better is to simply be an ordinary human being and be able to realize enlightenment. It is this amazing potential that makes our human birth a treasure of greater value than *anything*."

According to Buddhist tradition *this* is why we have been born human—not to become *Buddhists*, so much as to undertake the *practice* of being authentically ourselves, awake to the non-dual presence of bugs, trees, sun, moon, stars, mountains, rivers, earth and wind. This jataka says: "You can have whatever you've personally dreamed of—wealth, ease, comfort, pleasure, beauty, and long life, but no way of evolving, no way of realizing freedom from ego and fulfilling your deepest vows. Or, just as you are, with all your problems and issues, warts, as they say and all, you can choose to take up a Way of Liberation. The choice is yours. Which shall it be?"

In the Campeyya jataka, the Buddha, as the Bodhisattva in a distant past life, stood at this crossroads and learned the hard way what was important. Poverty-stricken, he chose riches and splendor over the pains of an all-too human life. Then he discovered that, from the perspective of his deepest vows, he'd made a mistake. While becoming a naga lord fulfilled his dreams of comfort and ease, there was a fly in the lavish ointment. As a naga he couldn't do what any ordinary human can—practice enlightenment. For that he'd have to become human again. *Oops*.

However, once he recognizes his mistake, he sets off to correct it and regain what he initially had, which is what we each now have and take so for granted—an ordinary human life. As the old saying goes: "Be careful what you wish for; you might get it." Mind-born wishes and desires generate power and, like vows, once set in actual motion, we must live out their consequences. The Bodhisattva's recognition of failure in this jataka of his birth as a naga, marks the re-awakening of his ancient Vow, said to have been made ages in the past. Back then he was a sage named Sumedha and in that long-ago time, world ages back, when he met the Buddha Dipankara, he was so inspired that he vowed not to just personally awaken and enter nirvana, but to become a full Buddha himself, able to guide all beings. (This tale is related in full in the *Niddankantha*—the formal introduction to the Pali *Jataka*.) The pain and regret he now feels, then, is positive. His ancient Vow reveals that he's drifted from his deepest intention. Losing and finding the Way is how bodhisattvas develop spiritual muscle, what Zen calls, "power for the Way." No sincere effort is wasted. All is grist for the Vow-mill.

The challenge of this fairytale-like jataka, and where its ego-killing venom lies, is in this: the treasure we truly seek is right where we are and it can be ours, *if* we don't let our chance go by. *But will we?* Will we use this rare and precious human life to embody our Vow, or will we fritter away our all too brief time here?

There's nothing at all wrong with satisfaction, yet how easy it is when seeking some personal heaven, to lose sight of our deeper potential. The core lesson of the Campeyya Jataka—that gaining the world can mean losing your soul—is universal. When Esau sells his birthright to his brother, Jacob, for a mess of pottage, the greater is lost for the sake of the lesser. Blake wrote, "More, more is the cry of a mistaken soul. Less than All cannot satisfy." (*There is No Natural Religion*.) Zen says, "Swallow all the water of the river in one gulp." In the end, the poor bodhisattva who'd so coveted wealth and splendor, renounces them completely, giving away so much treasure that the ground itself is turned the color of gold. He released literal wealth to gain the treasure we each now have and take so for granted: the treasure of human birth. Roshi Philip Kapleau, commenting on his initial enlightenment wrote, "But mostly, I am grateful for my human body, for the privilege to know this Joy like no other." (*The Three Pillars of Zen*)

The Campeyya Jataka reminds us that 2,500 years ago, back when it was first told, human beings already tended to overlook the treasure they had, and what they might do with it. "If you don't believe this is all true," the story even insists, "look at the golden-colored earth beneath your feet." Seeing is believing is a very simple, and clearly very old, storytelling device.

Let this jataka serve as our treasure map, revealing where X marks the spot. All we need do is roll up our sleeves and dig down, right where we are. The practice of Zen is how we uncover our treasure.

10

Bodhisattvas We Live Among: Plants, Trees, and Aspiration

> Trees are sanctuaries. Whoever knows how to speak to them, whoever knows how to listen to them, can learn the truth. They do not preach learning and precepts, they preach, undeterred by particulars, the ancient law of life.
> Hermann Hesse, *Wandering*

> As Frodo prepared to follow him, he laid his hand upon the tree beside the ladder: never before had he been so suddenly and so keenly aware of the feel and texture of a tree's skin and of the life within it. He felt a delight in wood and the touch of it, neither as forester nor as carpenter; it was the delight of the living tree itself.
> J.R.R. Tolkien, *The Lord of the Rings*

Buddhist legend says that the Buddha was born under sala trees; that as a young child he experienced deep samadhi while sitting alone beneath a rose-apple tree; that as a young man he realized full and perfect enlightenment seated under the Bodhi Tree; and that at life's end he lay down beneath twin sala trees and entered his parinirvana. Trees accompanied him, birth to death.

In jataka tales, trees and plants, like animals, nagas, ogres, gods, and humans have an inner spiritual life, and can be wise and compassionate. Trees that unselfconsciously consume carbon dioxide and release life-giving oxygen are the primal mothers and fathers of life on Earth. Indeed, once they were the most intelligent beings on Earth. They colonized and covered, spreading themselves over the land. Shattering rock into nutrient rich soil, slowly, patiently, they turned a barren planet into a garden. A haiku by Shiki captures the aliveness of plants:

> In the summer rains
> the creeping gourd
> has reached the trelliswork.

Yet perhaps because they remain rooted and cannot wander, we tend to think of plants and trees as mere ornaments, things with which to decorate our lawns and neighborhoods. Familiarity breeds not only contempt, but blindness. At best, perhaps we see trees and plants as useful sources of food, medicine, or supplies like rubber and turpentine. At worst, we see them as piles of lumber ready to convert into cash. Blake wrote, "A fool sees not the same tree that a wise man sees." (*The Marriage of Heaven and Hell*.) What does a wise person see when looking at a tree? Blake hinted at an answer in a letter he wrote in 1799 to the Reverend John Truster.: "The tree which moves some to tears of joy is in the eyes of others only a green thing which stands in the way."

The Buddhist jatakas remind us that trees are living beings. Like us they not only experience birth, aging, illness, and death, but may also have families. It seems that older trees in forests may shelter younger relatives, and younger trees may be actively keeping venerable stumps alive by directing nutrients their way. Trees and plants seem to share information via chemical and fungal pathways. A recent study even suggests that trees have a kind of pulse or heartbeat, only one so slow humans can't hear it.

There are jatakas in which the Buddha in a past life is a tree, or is the consciousness, or inner life of a tree; the *divinity* of the tree is how the jatakas put it. Though trees, unlike Tolkien's Ents, cannot go striding across the landscape, these jatakas suggest that trees might not only be aware of human good and evil, but might also be motivated—and able—to do something about it.

Here are several "tree jatakas." The first is the Bhadda-Kunala Jataka, number 465 in the Pali *Jataka* of 547 such past life tales. It essentially goes like this:

Long ago, the King of Benares wanted to create a palace that would be the envy of all the kings of India. Palaces needed many columns or pillars to support them, but his palace would be a marvel, for it would need only one pillar. To create the sole column capable of bearing the weight of the entire palace, a perfectly straight and absolutely massive tree would be required.

After some searching his workmen discovered the perfect tree; a Sal tree, growing in the king's own park. With the king's permission they gathered at the tree, lit incense and lamps, offered flowers, tied a cord around its trunk, and announced – "Seven days from now, O Great Tree, by royal decree you will be cut down. Let any deities dwelling in you go elsewhere. May they not blame us for destroying their home."

At that time, the Bodhisattva was the consciousness of that tree, its in-dwelling god or guiding spirit. Hearing these words he thought: "These workmen plan to cut down my tree. I live only as long as my tree lives. Plus, the young Sal trees growing nearby are my kin and many are my own children. When I fall they will be crushed and broken. Once the shelter and nourishment I provide them is gone, the young trees that survive will face hardship and death. I must stop this. I must protect them."

That very midnight the Bodhisattva appeared in the king's bedchamber. The king awoke to find his room bright with radiance and with a glowing god hovering at his bedside, weeping!. With hair standing on end in terror, the king stammered, "Who are you? And why, O Great Being, do you weep?"

Then the Bodhisattva, Lord of Trees, answered, "In your realm, O King, I am known as 'The Lucky Tree.' Considered sacred, I was worshipped and allowed to grow unharmed. In peace, my kin and children grew around me. But now as we are threatened, I have come to you. There is merit in friendship with trees, O, King, especially with trees in which divinity dwells. You should maintain the Old Ways and not cut me down."

The king answered, "But you are the greatest and strongest of trees. This is why I chose you to be the single pillar of my miraculous palace. As that pillar you will be honored through the ages. Of all trees, you will have attained a rare destiny."

The Tree Bodhisattva said, "I see it differently. The honor you plan to bestow on me means my death and the death of my family. If you insist on this then I ask one favor: cut me in pieces starting at the top, not the bottom. Cut the top, then the middle and, last of all, the root. If you do this, my death will not be so painful to me."

The king said, "What? Cut you from the top in pieces rather than all at once from the root? Such a death is reserved for the worst of criminals! O, Lucky Tree, why do you ask such a terrible thing?"

The Bodhisattva answered, "My family and children grow around me. Given my great size, if I fall in one piece many of them will be crushed, broken, or killed. I cannot allow it. I am their parent and protector. I must do all I can to spare them from harm. They will be saved if I am cut in sections starting at the top. This is why I choose such a death."

"This is a worthy and selfless being," thought the king. "He acts for the good of his kin and the welfare of others, even though it means greater harm to himself. My plan to build a one-column palace has consequences I did not foresee. In light of this Great Being's selflessness, my aim is shown as less than worthy."

Then the king said, "O Lucky Tree Divine Spirit! Your thoughts and aims are noble, greater than my own. Therefore I free you from my plan. You will not be cut down. My palace will not be built. May you and your kindred live on in peace. I renounce my childish vanity."

"My thanks, O King of Men," said the Tree Bodhisattva, who then vanished in a great blaze of green and golden light. The human king, filled with wonder for having spoken with such a divinity, gave gifts to his people, protected trees, and raised to a spirit of selflessness, did kind and generous deeds. At his death he entered higher realms.

After telling this tale the Buddha said, "The Tathagata, while no longer abiding within the household life, or within the lineage of kings, does not ignore his family but acts for their good and for the good of all. At that time, Ananda my cousin and attendant, was the human king, my present-day followers were the deities embodied in the young saplings, and I, myself, was The Lucky Tree, King of Tree Gods."

A wise person sees a different tree than a fool sees. The history behind this brief jataka is instructive. The tale was told by the Buddha after he'd tried three times to protect his birth-clan, the Shakyas, from destruction by their neighbors, the Licchavis. Each time war loomed he intervened. Yet in the end even he failed. No one evades the law of cause and effect. The Shakyas' heavy karma had ripened, and due to their own past actions they were decimated nearly to the point of extinction.

Here is a second brief jataka, number 334 in the Pali *Jataka*, The Rajovada Jataka:

Once a king wanted to find out where he stood with his people. Putting on a disguise he went out among them asking everyone what they thought of their king. One and all spoke the king's praises. The king thought, "How nice. But perhaps they don't speak the truth out of fear. Kings have been known to have spies. I will go to where sages dwell. They are honest. Perhaps one of them will reveal another truth."

At that time the Bodhisattva was a sage living high up in the Himalayas. Born into a Brahmin family, when he came of age and was educated in the arts of his rank, he left home to dedicate himself to spiritual practice. In time he realized higher awareness, and through realization, gained the attainments of equanimity, insight, compassion, and peace.

The Bodhisattva was sitting outside his meditation hut eating figs when the disguised king arrived. "Have some," said the Bodhisattva. The king ate the figs and found them sweet as sugar. He asked, "Why are these figs so sweet?" The Bodhisattva said, "They are so sweet because our king rules justly." The disguised king asked, "Would the figs lose their sweetness if the king were unjust?"

The Bodhisattva said, "If a king is unjust, then, oil, honey, molasses, wild roots, berries, fruits, and, yes, figs, all lose sweetness. The realm would be without flavor and the mind lose its joy. But when rulers are just, all things become sweet, and the realm rejoices."

Thanking the Bodhisattva, the king returned to Benares. Back in his palace he decided to test the truth of the Bodhisattva's words for himself. From then on he ruled unjustly. Months later he returned to the Bodhisattva, who again offered him a fig. He took a bite—and immediately spat it out. "It's bitter!" he exclaimed.

The Bodhisattva said, "Then our king is ruling unjustly. When rulers are unjust even the wild fruits of the forest know it."

The king thought, "His words are true. I will rule justly and make the figs sweet again." When he returned home he ruled justly, and the figs regained their original sweetness. After telling this jataka, the Buddha said, "At that time my faithful cousin and attendant, Ananda, was the king, and I was the ascetic."

Commentary

These two short, 2500 year-old jataka tales say that whatever humans do, or fail to do, affects other lives and life forms. In the first story, the king's desire to build a miraculous palace means death for some of the living beings we call "trees." (To share a bit of etymology, the English root for the word, "tree," is the same as for the word, "true.") The jataka of the disguised king repeats this same theme. The king's just reign brings sweetness even to the plants, while his unjust one sours the sweetest fruits—a vivid metaphor for the effects of human actions on other life forms.

The first jataka also reveals that trees have consciousness, an inner life, and are not just a series of mechanical processes. If so, perhaps a tree enjoys its sunlight as much as we enjoy sitting down to a hearty and delicious meal. Because trees are alive, they also grow, age, suffer illnesses, and die. The jataka adds that, as living beings, trees might also manifest bodhisattvic aspirations. They shelter many lives of many kinds of beings and provide food as well for countless living things; they share resources, communicate, remove pollutants from air and soil, and create the very oxygen that makes life possible here on Earth. (As well as make the living dirt that is "earth.") Doesn't this sound suspiciously ... bodhisattvic?

Our current reality is a troubled one, with much suffering, anxiety, alienation. While we remain an essentially optimistic species (Pandora keeps hope locked in the chest), nonetheless, after billions of years of rather astonishing evolution here on Earth, we now live in a sour, bitter world, much of it, alas, our own human doing. (The jataka of the consequence of unjust rule, seems rather to the point.) While we hope this will not be our final legacy, the clock is ticking. Perhaps the jatakas' ancient views can help us re-imagine our world, and rejoin the community of living things from which we've isolated ourselves to such catastrophic effect. It need not always be so. The potential to see through our blindness and its consequences is always there. To refer back to "Manjusri's 3x3 front, 3x3 back," this option remains undiminished, and is always open to us. In fact, a Buddhist legend says that despite our current problems we live in the *Bhadra*, or "Fortunate" kalpa. Why? Because in our time, perhaps given the very extremity of our situation, a thousand bodhisattvas will spring up from the earth, emerging from the ground itself like a forest of ... trees.

11

The Bodhisattva Saves the Realm— as the Consciousness of a Tree

Jataka 520, the Ganatindu Jataka, looks not only at the mind but the bodhisattvic *activity* of trees, and explores further the issue of the "souring" of the world created by human injustice. Here's the tale:

Long ago in the kingdom of Kampila, a city of the Northern Pancalas, a king named Pancala ruled selfishly. His ministers, following their king's lead, were self-centered as well. The villagers who were his subjects, oppressed by the heavy taxation meant to line the king's and his minister's pockets, hid in the forests during daylight to avoid the tax collectors. At night when they returned they had to drag away the thorn branches they'd piled round their windows and doors to secure their homes from robbers. All bore deep cuts, scratches, and wounds from the thorns.

At that time, the Bodhisattva came to life as the divinity of a sacred medicinal tinduka tree, one long known for its healing powers. This tree grew just outside the walls of the capital city, and once a year following ancient custom, King Pancala would go to this tree and there make an offering of a thousand pieces of money seeking the tree's protection over his reign and realm.

The Bodhisattva Divinity of that tree thought, "Though the king honors me, his kingdom is falling into ruin and he does not see it. I must protect the realm. No one else can do it. I will make his error clear. He respects no one, but will listen to me."

That night the Bodhisattva appeared in the king's bedchamber. The king awoke, and terrified to find a great burning apparition at his bedside, stammered out, "Who are you radiating such glory? And why are you here?"

"O King, I am the Divinity of the Tinduka Tree," said the Bodhisattva in a voice of majesty and power. "Do not fear. I have come out of compassion for you. Because you are ruling unwisely your kingdom is falling into ruin. Selfishness spreads and such is its power, it can destroy entire realms. To guard against this, a king must be careful. Attention is what lays the foundations of long and successful rule." Then he spoke in verse:

> Eagerness for the Way is the Path to Nirvana,
> Lack of attention brings death.
> Vigilant beings find life,
> But the careless die while living.
> From pride comes sloth: from sloth comes loss.
> Put away sloth, O King. Put away self-centeredness!
> How many kings have lost both
> Wealth and realm through selfishness.
>
> The wheel of karma ever turns.
> Those who are up high today
> Fall low tomorrow.
>
> You've handed your realm to robbers.
> Your sons will not inherit your wealth.
> Your realm will be taken.
>
> Regain the Path.
> Ruling well, true riches increase.
> It is not too late!
>
> Open your eyes and ears!
> Learn what your people say.

The Bodhisattva Saves the Realm

This is my advice.
No one can offer more.

Having spoken, the blazing apparition vanished. Shaken by his divine encounter, the king lay wakeful through the night. Come morning he put on the clothes of an ordinary man, gave his kingdom over to the care of his ministers, and accompanied by his closest advisor, the chaplain, left the city determined to uncover the truth or falsity of his uncanny encounter for himself.

In a distant village they saw a man pile thorn branches around his house, then set off with his wife and children into the forest. When the taxmen arrived they found the village deserted, thorn branches piled around every home. In the evening when the taxmen departed, the villagers returned. Pulling the thorn branches away from his door, the man they'd seen earlier gave a howl of pain, then sat down and pulled out a large thorn that had pierced his foot. Then, inspired by the watchful presence of the Tree Bodhisattva, he cursed the king in verse!

May the king be pierced by an arrow in some fray,
As I've been pierced by this thorn today.
May Pancala mourn for wounding me
With the sharp thorn of this thorn tree.

The chaplain said, "Why do you blame the king? You yourself stepped on the thorn. Surely the error is yours." But again, given words in verse by the Tree Bodhisattva, the man answered –

Because of the king I feel such pain.
Defenseless folk by oppressors are slain.
By night, thieves prey on us, then it's tax collectors
   by day.

> Vicious folks run the realm when evil kings hold sway.
> Distressed by fear to the forest we flee,
> And pile thorns round our homes for security.

The disguised king thought "He has a point. Without the one, then not the other." And he said to the chaplain, "I have been warned. Disaster approaches. Let us return. I must rule righteously." But the Bodhisattva inspired the chaplain to say, "Great king, it may be so. Or it may not. Let us go on and be sure. Certainly there are gods, but there are also tricksters."

In another village, they saw a poorly dressed woman struggling under a load of firewood. Though she had two grown daughters, she would not let them go into the woods to gather firewood without husbands to protect them from wild beasts and men. Now under her heavy load, she stumbled and fell. In pain, inspired by the presence of the Tree Bodhisattva, she too, cursed the king.

> When will this King Pancala die?
> For unwed daughters' sakes I cry!
> As long as he reigns
> They will sigh
> For husbands and children in vain.

The chaplain said, "Foolish words are meritless! Is the king a matchmaker?" But given words by the watchful Bodhisattva, she answered:

> My words were not vain,
> When defenseless folk
> By oppressors are slain.
> At night we're prey to thieves.
> Then it's greedy men by day.

> Bad people run the show
> When evil kings hold sway.
> In such times how can poor girls
> Hope to wed?
> Our lives will not improve
> Until this king is dead!

The king thought, "She's not wrong. My people suffer. As I am the king, what I do is at root."

They next encountered a plowman whose ox had been struck and wounded by the plow. In verse he, too, inspired by the Tree Bodhisattva, cursed the king.

> So may our king fall, speared by some foe,
> As my injured ox has fallen and lies low.

The chaplain said, "Why blame the king? You hit your ox with your own plow. Your carelessness is at root, not his." But guided by the Tree Bodhisattva, the plowman answered:

> I'm angry with the king and rightly so, I claim.
> When defenseless folk are by oppressors slain.
> By night thieves prey on us, by day it's the king's own men,
> Who stole my lunch. To get me more, my wife had to run.
> While I worked on faint, I slipped.
> And so my ox's leg was ripped.

"What I do – or fail to do," thought the king, "harms people and animals alike."

Next they met a man who'd tried to milk a wild buffalo cow and been trampled. In agony he, too, cursed the king:

> May our wretched king fall in some fray,
> As I am laid low because of him today.

The chaplain said, "How is your injury the king's fault?" Inspired by the Bodhisattva, the man replied:

> The king's to blame, for in his reign
> Defenseless folk are by oppressors slain.
> At night it's thieves; by day his men harass us sore.
> They took my cow, while demands for milk grew more.
> Desperate, a buffalo cow I tried to milk today.
> Now badly hurt, my curse I'll say.

The chaplain and king each said, "There is a connection," and turned for home. Passing through a village, they learned that a tax collector had just slaughtered a dappled calf to make a pretty sword sheath of its hide. The calf's mother was roaming the village bawling and lamenting, unwilling to eat or drink for grief. Even the callous village boys were moved, and guided to poetry by the Bodhisattva of the Medicine Tree, cursed the king:

> Let our now king pine and his children weep in vain,
> Like this poor cow, whose calf his men have slain.

The chaplain said, "How is this the king's fault?" The boys answered:

> By night we're prey to thieves, then it's the king's men
>   by day.

Brutal folk have license when evil kings hold sway.
Should a still nursing calf be slain to make a pretty
   sword sheath?
Tell us, pray!

The king said, "There was no call for such brutality."

Nearing the capital city, they passed a nearly dry water tank where crows were gathering to stab frogs with their beaks, and eat them. By the power of great compassion, the Bodhisattva cursed the king from the mouth of a frog:

So may our king in fight be beaten, sons and all,
As we woodland frogs to village crows now fall.

The chaplain said, "Can kings guard every creature? Crows eat frogs. This is only natural. Surely this can't be blamed on the king!"

But guided by the Bodhisattva, the frog answered:

Your words are flattering,
And will deceive the king.
If blest with prosperity
This realm would peaceful be,
Crows as village birds, good offerings would enjoy.
And have no need, our lives to destroy.

The king said, "All creatures, down to the frogs in the slime in the drying water tanks now suffer. It must end. Giving in to selfishness, I lost the Way. The Tree Divinity was right; I must change my life and bring benefit, not harm, to my subjects, down even to the frogs in the water tanks."

When they returned, this is what he did. And in time the realm again prospered.

At the conclusion of this jataka the Buddha said, "A leader must forsake evil courses and rule for the benefit of all. If he does, his realm will prosper. In that long ago time, I myself was the divinity of the Tinduka Tree."

Commentary

The jataka of the Tinduka Tree presents a familiar enough story: the state rots from the top down. The responsibilities of leadership are at least as great if not greater than the perks—as anyone who's held a position of responsibility knows. There are always consequences. Parents must accept the uncomfortable knowledge that children model themselves not on what the parents say, but on what they do.

A side-note: in this jataka, the presence of the Bodhisattva is signaled when ordinary human—and non-human—beings, spontaneously burst into verse as if singing their lines. In the presence of the gods, it seems, we rise to higher levels. Have we uncovered the ancient roots of opera and musical comedy? Of course, casting curses traditionally depended on some skill with rhyme and poetry to make it "stick." (And hopefully offer counter-protection, as well—"Sticks and stones may break my bones, but words can never harm me.") Interestingly, in the Pali *Jataka* it is the verses not the narrative, that are regarded as canonical.

Regardless, in this 2500-year-old tale we are asked to open ourselves to a wider-than-usual view. The jataka says that not only can a tree can be conscious, but it can be a bodhisattva with the power to intervene in human affairs and act over a distance, to do good, avoid evil, and save the many beings, and so fulfill the three traditional "general resolutions" of all wisdom beings.

Can there be any truth to this? Actually, scientists are now contemplating whether trees, in partnership with fungi, might not form a "wood-wide-web" of global inter-communication. While this remains speculative—so far—what is clear is that trees shelter birds, squirrels, beetles, ants, raccoons, larvae, mosses, lizards, grubs, lichens, and fungi, remove carbon dioxide from the air, pollutants from the soil, pump oxygen into the atmosphere and, through transpiration, cool the atmosphere and, so, help in reducing global warming. In death, they decay into pulp, continue to add nutrients to the soil and host many various lifeforms. Plus, like all green plants, they photosynthesize life energy directly from sunlight, and have no need to kill to live. How's that for ahimsa or non-harming? Like whales and dolphins, trees give off the markings of compassion. Why shouldn't we accept that they can or might be, bodhisattvas? And there's this:

> You and the tree in your backyard come from a common ancestor. A billion and a half years ago, the two of you parted ways. But even now, after an immense journey in separate directions, that tree and you still share a quarter of your genes.
> Richard Powers, *The Overstory: A Novel*

In *The Overstory*, Powers also draws on experiments by Canadian ecologist, Suzanne Simard, in which she concludes that plants form communities and guilds and that they communicate with one another chemically, as well as across species. Her central point is that trees care for one another—to paraphrase Jill Lepore's summation in ""What We Owe Our Trees," *New Yorker*, 5/29/2023. To continue with what Lepore says:

> The trees under attack pump out insecticides to save their lives. That much is uncontroversial. But something else in the data makes her flesh pucker: trees a little way off, untouched by the invading swarms, ramp up their own defenses when their neighbor is attacked.

> Something *alerts* them. They get wind of the disaster, and they prepare. She controls for everything she can, and the results are always the same. Only one conclusion makes any sense: The wounded trees send out alarms that other trees smell. Her maples are *signaling*.

And:

> In the past ten thousand years, the Earth has lost about a third of its forest, which wouldn't be so worrying if it weren't for the fact that all that loss has happened in the past three hundred years or so. As much forest has been lost in the past hundred years as in the nine thousand before.

Yet, sadly, globally we're still indiscriminately cutting down the very beings whose help we may soon almost desperately need. With fewer trees and forests storing carbon, releasing oxygen, stabilizing habitats, future generations may be in for an increasingly rough ride. As Lepore also says, "Forests fed us, housed us, and made our way of life possible. But they can't save us if we can't save them."

The Talmud says that each blade of grass has its own angel hovering over it, whispering "Grow! Grow!" In this jataka, the Bodhisattva tree divinity extends its encouragement well beyond the vicinity of its own tree. Yet even if a tree or the consciousness of a tree wanted to do this, could it? Beyond offering fruits, sap, leaves and bark as food and medicine, providing shelter, and via fungal networks and root systems, sending warnings to other trees, how could a tree actually help? They are mobile to a limited extent. Root tips avoid obstacles and seek water, leaves turn toward sunlight, and chemical messages spread along root and fungal networks. But this all takes place slowly compared to the nervy quickness of animals. How could a tree fulfill bodhisattva vows to "do good, avoid evil, and save the many beings"? How could it help anyone or anything not in its immediate vicinity? Yet in this jataka, the Buddha in a past life as the bodhisattvic consciousness of a tree, demonstrates both wide-ranging awareness, as well as an ability to influence events at a distance.

Oddly, such broad awareness and an ability to act at a distance as imagined in this 2500 year-old jataka tale, *could* be something a tree—the conscious being we call "tree"—might actually have. After all, through its roots, leaves, and fungal webs, a tree is woven into the living fabric of forest and city, into the body of the Earth, as well as endlessly up and up into the undying light of sun, moon, and stars. Wu-men's verse to case 20 of *The Gateless Barrier*, is not at all about a tree but could, nonetheless, be easily applied to one:

> Lifting my leg I kick up the Scented Ocean,
> Lowering my head, I look down on the Four Dhyana
> > Heavens.
> My body is so big there is no place to put it.

If we take off habitual blinders and really look at a tree, we might find ourselves rather puzzled: where *does* its body and consciousness end? Woven into a network of living awareness, a tree bodhisattva—assuming that there are such beings—might, indeed, be able to encourage the budding of wisdom at a distance—as we see in this tale. Here the Tree Bodhisattva's actions, while not overt, are skillful, capable of quietly inspiring significant life changes. Isn't this what real teaching comes down to? Wisdom can't be *given* to anyone. But contexts through which there is a greater than statistical likelihood of its arising, can be created and nurtured. Wisdom can be planted. Compassionate action can water the seed and help it grow.

Yet at the start of the jataka, the Bodhisattva is not so subtle. Instead he steps up, and presenting himself as a great blaze of light, straightforwardly intercedes, quite unequivocally and directly, saying "Don't do that!" It is only after this dramatic entrance that he begins stage-managing behind the scenes, encouraging the good that does not yet exist to arise. In short, he works to stop evil, do good, and save the many beings. As a tree!

The king never knows that a bodhisattva is behind all his seemingly chance encounters. Nor does he suspect that the bodhisattva involved is the guiding spirit of his own honored tinduka tree. All he knows is that a tree divinity appeared and told him to stop harming himself and his realm. In setting out to verify what he's been told, we see his potential. He must confirm the truth or falseness of even a divinity's words for himself. In this way, he establishes a solid foundation for lasting change. Rather than just doing as he's been told, even by so potent an authority as a higher power, or simply reacting in fear to a supernatural warning, he finds personal truth to be his best motivation. Good for him!

And yet, there is more at work. For the Tree Bodhisattva doesn't just set things in motion and leave. ("I did what I could. Now it's up to him.") He follows through, doing all he can to help this king find his way to a wise change of heart. He is also providing us (and all who encounter the tale), with a model of how to *live* the Path.

We, too, need not draw attention to ourselves to fulfill the three general resolutions upheld by all maturing bodhisattvas. We, too, can find ways to act quietly, and yet be skillful and effective. A kind word, an outstretched hand create possibilities; as does washing the extra dish, going the extra mile, or offering a moment of loving-kindness. Or simply being present for a moment in the midst of our day, present with Mu, with this breath, this count, this koan and, then, coming forward from there into whatever's on our plate. Remaining hidden and invisible is not the point; being effective and helpful is. We, too, can follow through, mean what we say, and act on what we recognize as important to more than just ourselves and our own interests. We, too, can find ways to think and act for the welfare of others, of all. It comes down to commitment and integrity; it comes down to Vows.

Perhaps the Tree Bodhisattva is not unique. Silently flourishing, harmlessly drawing energy from sun, soil, and water, trees are not necessarily passive but may, as the jatakas show, be doing all they can to nurture life and be of help. Unfortunately, we humans are not paying such good attention. If only a tree spirit would rise up like some great burning bush in the bedrooms of CEOs, presidents, and kings, maybe things would change.

Through ongoing, moment-to-moment Zen practice-realization, we, too, can align ourselves with the fundamental Goodness (with a capital "G") that sustains living things. In simple, ordinary, intimate ways we can work like trees for the benefit of all, even as we work as well for the liberation of trees, bushes, and grasses. Buddhist tradition makes this explicit, holding that bodhisattvas vow not to enter nirvana until all beings, down to every last bush and blade of grass, have realized complete and perfect enlightenment. Right now, with this breath, this koan, this moment of life, not off in some ideal future, is how and where that commitment takes root. If it is our intention, our vow, to benefit others, then little by little if we keep at it, skills improve and tiny actions add up to tipping points.

For the king and his chaplain the horror of the little calf's slaughter is one such tipping point. (If cows were sacred in India 2,500 years ago when this tale was first told, then that horror would be compounded.) The magical conversation with the frog, so far beyond whatever might be considered as rational, is another. The entire realm and all its many beings groan for liberation from one man's—the king's—self-centeredness. Through the compassionately skillful intervention of the bodhisattvic consciousness of a tree, the king comes to know this as personal truth. When he returns home, he is a new man, someone who recognizes his own power to transform the kingdom to the good. Which happens because the consciousness of a tree chose to act on its aspiration to shelter the realm. And it also happens because the king himself has left one small door open to something beyond himself; it happens because he holds the tinduka tree to be sacred. Through this little opening, this faith, innate Goodness has a chance to flow. The king's regard for the tree makes his own transformation possible.

A Zen teacher once said, "I want to become a great shade tree, able to shelter all beings." Zen master Dogen wrote, "In the assemblies of the enlightened ones there have been many cases of mastering the Way bringing forth the heart of plants and trees; this is what awakening the mind for enlightenment is like." ("Awakening the Unsurpassed Mind," *Shobogenzo*.) Lin-ji was planting pine trees when his teacher, Huang-po, asked, "What's the good of planting so many trees in the deep mountains?" Lin-chi answered, "First, I want to beautify the natural setting of the main gate. Second, I want to leave something to inspire future generations."

Counting each breath, experiencing each breath, questioning a koan, re-affirming and taking to heart Great Vows for All, is our work of planting saplings and putting down roots for future generations. Little by little, breath-by-breath, koan-by-koan, sesshin-by-sesshin, dokusan-by-dokusan we give up our habitual commitment to self-centeredness. The moment-by-moment decision to attend to the practice, rather than to old, habitual, mental-emotional loops is a choice, never a given. Setting aside time each day to sit in zazen, is a beneficial, bodhisattvic habit. But the practice of realization itself, which is what happens in zazen, is *not* habitual. It is *just* this breath, this count, this koan, without before or after. Each is complete each time. There's nothing to compare this breath, this count, this moment of Mu to, no way to know it in *relation* to anything else. Each is fresh and new each time. As we give attention to this count of *one*, this *two*, this *three*, this breath, this koan, the wind in the trees confirms us, the *Caw!* of the crow, the *Woof!* of the dog, the *vroom* of the car confirms us; each is *It.* Just as we are, we touch base with boundless life. The prison of habitual, unconscious self-centeredness falls away.

Recognizing the harmful effects—even to oneself—of self-centered thoughts and behaviors can, at the right time, become its own impetus to maturing—as in this jataka, when the king at last sees the effects of his own thoughts and deeds. Triggered by the Bodhisattva's initially dramatic appearance, then nudged along by the Bodhisattva's hidden efforts, he is eventually convinced and transformed. Emperor Ashoka (268-232 BCE) toured a battlefield shortly after one of his great military victories. Triumphant at the start, he became appalled by the carnage and suffering he saw around him, all of which he himself had inflicted. Not long afterward he converted to Buddhism, and his subsequent edicts, carved on stone pillars throughout the Indian subcontinent, served as guides toward an ethical and peaceful life.

How do we live *our* vows in difficult times? One fundamental response, and a good one, is Zen practice itself. Don't think you're doing nothing by sitting in silence, doing zazen. Zen Master Dogen, in the "Bendowa" ("Negotiation of the Way") section of the *Shobogenzo* reminds us:

> ... the zazen of even one person at one moment imperceptibly accords with all things and fully resonates through all time. Thus, in the past, future, and present of the limitless universe, this zazen carries on the buddha's transformation endlessly and timelessly. Each moment of zazen is equally the wholeness of practice, equally the wholeness of realization. This is so not only while sitting; like a hammer striking emptiness, before and after its

exquisite sound permeates everywhere. How can it be limited to this time and space?

Myriad beings all manifest original practice, original face; it is impossible to measure. Even if all buddhas of the ten directions, as innumerable as the sands of the Ganges, exert their strength and with the buddha wisdom try to measure the merit of one person's zazen, they will not be able to fully comprehend it.

Of course, it is equally true that the actions of one person committed to self-centeredness, to advancing their own precious self above all else, will rend the social fabric, as the jatakas also show. If deep down you think you are not connected, that you stand alone, an isolated, hard-edged ego, you might want to look again. Our ordinary life and our own times proclaim the truth of interconnection sometimes joyously, sometimes painfully. The Internet has sped up this recognition. We easily see how what happens "over there" affects us "over here" and vice versa. Nothing is separate and alone. Continuing to sell off the Amazon's trees for lumber or to create grazing land for cattle literally makes us short of breath. Zen presents this understanding intimately. Using contemporary Western names rather than ancient Chinese ones, a Zen saying might now go: "When Alice drinks in Rochester, Sam gets tipsy in Chicago."

After realizing intimacy with the morning star, the Buddha did not stay quietly seated beneath the Bodhi tree. After three weeks of total absorption in the joy of complete liberation, he got up, set off along the dusty roads of India, selflessly teaching all he met. This need not be a big deal. Basho, near death, wrote:

Deep autumn—
my neighbor,
how does he live, I wonder?

Even at such a moment he thought of the guy down the road: "How does he manage in this life?"

Traditional peoples worldwide hold that the natural world is conscious, that non-human beings are aware of what we humans do, and what we fail to do. Ecology confirms the reality of mutual interconnection. While what other living beings do and think affects us, given our technological prowess, what we think and do, has such power that it can bring benefit or harm to all living things, bacteria to blue whale, algae to redwoods. Being human, becoming human, is an awesome privilege, and given the weight we can throw around, carries serious responsibilities. Having attained a precious human birth how shall we use our opportunity—and our power?

Perhaps the natural world is signaling us almost desperately, reminding us of how intimate our mutual interconnections are, reminding us, too, that our current sense of entitled isolation is harmful to all. Our planet's story is not told in words but in events—melting glaciers, dying forests, vanishing species, expanding deserts, rising oceans—all of which make it terribly clear that our own thoughts and deeds have consequences. In light of this, even thinking about or simply reciting bodhisattva vows, Great Vows for All or the Four Vows, has significance. It's a start, an affirmation of something vital. "In dreams begin responsibilities,"as Yeats said. To return to the words of the San (Bushmen), it is not only our dream, for "There is a dream dreaming us." Zen master Dogen wrote, "The sutras are the entire universe, mountains and rivers and the great earth, plants and trees ..." ("The Samadhi of Self-enlightenment," Kim, *Eihei Dogen: Mystical Realist*)

Life is short. Time waits for no one. Will we grow-up in time? It starts with deciding that we want to, and that we *should*. This Path of maturing is what Buddhism calls "the Way of the Bodhisattva." Remove the esoteric trappings and cultural accretions and the "Way of the Bodhisattva" becomes the Way of the Growing-up Being, someone wisely choosing to mature beyond their own habitually unconscious self-centeredness. Being selfless does not mean a loss or lack. You don't become a zombie, a mindless thing with no self, no center. Look at the writings and doings of some of the old Zen masters and what you see is tremendously vital character and independence, creativity and compassion. The loss Zen speaks about, this "Great Death," is not a literal loss at all. Or rather, it's the loss of what was never needed from the start, a loss of the ignorance, greed and selfishness that inevitably comes from misunderstanding our own nature.

Such a loss is our greatest gain. The world and its beings step in, and we re-find our original body. Like a tree, we too are woven into the great web of life, our body so big, there's no place to put it. Once we "get" this, then, like the 11-headed, 1,000-armed bodhisattva, we can roll up our sleeves and get to work.

Section 3

The Way of the Ordinary Bodhisattva

12

A Pillar of Zen: Memorial for Roshi Philip Kapleau

This, my personal remembrance of Roshi Philip Kapleau, originally appeared in the September 2004 issue of *Buddhadharma: The Practitioner's Quarterly*, the first issue after his death in May of that year. Why have I included it here? Let me offer some context.

Roshi Kapleau was my root teacher. We were together from 1970 until his death in 2004, originally as teacher and student, then as master and disciple, then eventually as something much more intimate, like family. We were friends, and as friends, we did things together—travel, movies, restaurants, museums, meals and conversation. He changed my life for the good. Yet he was not a perfect, radiant, obviously bodhisattvic person. He had his issues. He had his flaws. I knew it. He knew it. He could be stubborn, short-sighted, blind and tough. Yet he never wavered from trying his best, even when that best meant falling down, getting back up, and trying again. In his dedication to Zen practice and teaching, despite his flaws, he embodied a way of being a sincere, yet ordinary bodhisattva, something that I and others, too, found to be of a most rare and genuine value. Rather extraordinary, after all.

So ... A Pillar of Zen.

My Zen teacher, Roshi Philip Kapleau, died peacefully on May 6, 2004 at the venerable age of 91. Several days later, many of us who had known him and been with him for more than thirty years gathered for his burial at the Chapin Mill Retreat Center, the country property of Rochester Zen Center. Some who were there had since found other teachers and other teachings, or had simply taken other directions in life than the path of Zen. All of us, though, felt a deep gratitude and love that no words can express.

Each person there seemed to find that at bottom they owed this man so much. He had opened the gate of practice, and his immense love of the dharma had saved us from deeply painful lives. *The Three Pillars of Zen*—the now classic work that brought him into the public eye and led him to found the first Zen center in America headed by a Westerner—was published in 1965, when the world was in chaos, the Vietnam War still on. Most of us were only in our early twenties, and somewhat crazed. He stood at an ancient door, held it open wide, and said to us simply, "Come in. Work hard. The dharma will never let you down."

Roshi's dying and death occurred outdoors, beneath the new-leaved trees in the backyard of the Rochester Zen Center, where some thirty years earlier he and a cadre of quite unskilled laborers had built this center from a burnt-out shell of a building. (He liked to say in those early days, "We specialize in burnt-out buildings and people.") Spring had just come to the Northeast, so the birds sang and the sun shone down to where he sat in his wheelchair—like the Buddha beneath the flowering sala trees. He wore his favorite chinos, flannel shirt, tan cloth sneakers and sunglasses, and was surrounded by friends, some from Rochester, others who had flown in to be with him. He had been living with Parkinson's the last thirteen years, living admirably actually, but getting weaker and weaker, especially this last year. The last few days he also had pneumonia. It was time to go.

His mind had remained clear and he still loved jokes, though even his favorite movies—Mel Brooks's *To Be or Not to Be*, *Ninotchka* and *Fiddler on The Roof* among them—had, over the last several months, become hard for him to follow. (He had recently taken, too, to watching only the first half of *Fiddler*; the second part now seemed too sad.) Each scene was compelling for him but putting the narrative together had gotten tricky. He still loved to laugh and to be read to, everything from koans and koan commentaries, poetry, history, politics, news and science to *The Cat Who Went to Heaven*, one of his favorites, and *Horton Hatches the Egg*—which he pronounced a great Zen tale, one that all Zen students should read.

Slowly, slowly as far-off dharma friends called and the phone was held to his ear to receive their well wishes and farewells, he drifted further away. His eyes had closed earlier and now, as death approached, his breathing simply became ever fainter and shallower. The passage between life and death was so subtle and gentle it is hard to pinpoint when death actually occurred. An exhale. Another. Then he was off, between breaths and worlds.

Friends sat with him still, whispering into his ear, holding his hand. And there was chanting—the Prajna Paramita, Sho Sai Myo, and Kanzeon. That night the local Zen community and many longtime friends gathered in the zendo. Two of his closest friends and students,

Sunyana Graef Sensei [now Roshi] and Rose Martin, had washed his body and clothed him in his rakusu and robes, and now he lay in an open casket before the altar. Over the next few days his un-embalmed body would show no signs of either rigor or decomposition.

He was buried, not cremated, by his own choice. When the notion was presented to him, he concurred that the decision for burial was not simply a personal preference but a dharma teaching. Form and essence are not-two. To burn the form would suggest that they are somehow separate. He would not accept that as an answer in dokusan. He did not embody it as a teaching now. Perhaps he was also saying that as Westerners and Buddhists we need not take on Eastern cultural forms. Our grandparents and parents were all buried. To be Buddhist need not mean we become anything other than what we already are. Let the natural processes proceed and the body decompose as the bodies of our ancestors and forebears had been allowed to do in their time. There is nothing to add to what we already are. Nothing special to do.

Philip Kapleau was born in 1912 to a working class family in New Haven, Connecticut. According to the Rochester Zen Center's obituary (the full copy of which may be seen on the center's Web site), as a young man he studied law and became a court reporter, serving for many years in the state and federal courts of Connecticut. He recorded trials of increasing importance and was selected in 1945 to serve as chief court reporter for the International Military Tribunal at Nuremberg. He later covered the Tokyo War Crimes Trials. His karma was unfolding, for in that unique position he took down testimony and became a witness to the greatest horrors not only of this last century, but, perhaps, of any. It was that horrifying experience that brought him to Zen. He used to say that two things about Japan affected him deeply. The first was the fact that the Japanese he met, unlike the Germans, were immediately willing to accept that their own sufferings had been caused by the suffering they had inflicted on others. It is our self-created karma,

Memorial for Roshi Philip Kapleau

he was told. And he was deeply moved by the great peace and stillness he experienced walking beneath the beautiful trees at many of the Zen temples he visited while in Japan for the trials.

He first took up Zen by reading voraciously in the literature available at the time, and by going to lectures and courses given by D.T. Suzuki at Columbia University. Beside writers, artists, musicians (like John Cage), and psychologists, there he sat, an American businessman, owner of a successful court-reporting firm.

Eventually finding Zen philosophy by itself of little use in solving the great malaise he felt after the war, in 1953 he sold his court-reporting business and returned to Japan to enter a Zen monastery and actually train in Zen, which he would do there for thirteen years. Early on, Soen Nakagawa-roshi became his friend. They called themselves "the two hobos" and it was Soen Nakagawa—brilliant, poetic, eccentric—who first took him under his wing, helped him find an entrance into the world of practice, and eventually introduced him to Harada-roshi, stern abbot of Hosshin-ji, saying "He will be a much better teacher for you, Kapleau-san."

Roshi Kapleau used to say that if it hadn't been for that initial generous and warm friendship with Nakagawa Roshi, the talks and travels, the hours they spent listening to recordings of Beethoven together, he might never have been able to stay in Japan or enter Zen at all. After three years of exhausting, miserable work under Harada Roshi, the great taskmaster of enlightenment, he continued his ongoing training as a layman with Yasutani Roshi. In the more relaxed atmosphere of that dedicated community of lay practitioners, he flourished. He "got" kensho. He married, had a child, and in 1965 was ordained as a Zen priest and sanctioned to begin teaching in the Harada-Yasutani line of Zen, which was to become so important and influential in the West.

While practicing under Yasutani Roshi he put his writing and court reporter skills to work, transcribing Zen teachers' talks, interviewing

Zen lay students and monks, and recording the practical details of Zen Buddhist practice. He was the first Westerner allowed to observe and record dokusan. The resulting book, *The Three Pillars of Zen*, was published in 1965 and quickly became the standard introductory text on Zen practice. It is still in print and has been translated into twelve languages. The story of the American ex-businessman in *The Three Pillars of Zen* is Roshi Kapleau's own enlightenment account, and it is still a corker, resonant and stirring. It tells you, better than any remembrance, why people flocked to the center he established in Rochester. Indeed, over the years, that one book opened wide the floodgate of practice for thousands of Western Zen students at Zen Centers throughout North and South America, Europe, Australia and New Zealand, and is still a vital, living work.

Two of the earliest readers of *The Three Pillars* were Ralph Chapin of Chapin Manufacturing in Batavia, New York, and Dorris Carlson of Rochester, the wife of Chester Carlson, the inventor of xerography, the technology that became the foundation for the Xerox Corporation. During his book tour in 1965, Dorris Carlson invited Roshi to visit her small meditation group and in June 1966, with the support of the Carlsons, he founded the Rochester Zen Center. These were not naïve, starry-eyed seekers but solid, mature and steady people. Perhaps they saw in Roshi what my father saw. When I told my father, now eighty-six himself, that Roshi had died he said, "Oh, I'm sorry to hear that. He was so down to earth, so kind and always such a gentleman." He was.

Though he could also be tough as nails—sometimes when you didn't want him to be—and sprout horns and fangs to reveal, in Zen parlance, the "black piercing eyes of a devil," he could also be as sweet and gentle and subtle and sensitive and wonderfully able to bless with his presence as a spring breeze after harshest winter. He had his particular failures and shortcomings. Sometimes his maverick strength (that firm, unyielding jaw and solid chin were perfectly made for stubbornly sticking out into the wind) was, at the same time, his greatest weakness. But given time and opportunity, he would invariably confess sorrow about his failures. "We all do stupid things sometimes," is what he told a dharma friend. And by that he meant himself; that *he* did stupid things and that he regretted them. Once he had a turkey brought into the Buddha Hall at Thanksgiving. It had been purchased by the Zen Center to be released, but now the bewildered bird flapped about anxiously. Roshi got us all chanting and, sure enough, the frightened bird grew calm. Then Roshi put his hands together and bowed deeply to the turkey in gassho style saying, "Turkey bows to turkey." He meant it. He had a knack for making waves. His style was to call a spade "a damn shovel!" He broke with his own teacher, Yasutani Roshi, as he said in *Zen: Merging of East and West* because of differences over the personalizing and Westernizing of Japanese Zen. Years later, after Yasutani Roshi's death, he said, with the greatest humility and sorrow, "If my old teacher should walk into this room now I would get down on my knees before him and beg for his forgiveness."

He could be mischievous, direct and down to earth. I remember after having dinner at his favorite local Chinese restaurant, we had a choice—we could go to a crowded, upscale cultural event, an opening at the museum, or we could head back to our house, my wife's and mine, and watch *Casablanca* together again, as we often did. We looked at each other. "Let's watch the movie!" he exclaimed. And we did, repeating joyfully in unison "Play it again, Sam!" He often chose intimacy over a crowd, and easy friendship on familiar ground over the social, dress-up affair. But he was no recluse. He also could love crowds, throwing himself into conversation and social whirl with child-like abandon, only stopping when someone noticed he was near collapse with exhaustion and dragged him away. He would have *loved* his own funeral services and his burial. They provided the very combination of pageantry, ceremony, community and socializing he so enjoyed. He had a committed sweet tooth, so chocolate bars were put in his coffin, along with small Buddhas, a leaf from the Bo tree, a long-life pill, which a practitioner had received from a Tibetan lama, and a harmonica. He loved to play the harmonica and had a number of old favorites, like Home on the Range and Auld Lang Syne, with which he'd turn sangha get-togethers into wonderful sing-alongs. For many years the Japanese bath was one of his greatest joys and he always had one in his quarters or nearby. Later he made it a practice to come to our house, where he liked to stretch out in our bigger, Japanese-style wooden tub, relax in very hot water (a metaphor for his life, when you think about it) and look up through the skylight into the trees. I also just recently learned from a dharma sister that he used to sometimes dance alone in his quarters when no one was around. She found this out when bringing him his afternoon tea. She would open the door—and there he might be, silently dancing to a beat all his own.

A great lover of animals, he dedicated his book on vegetarianism, *To Cherish All Life*, in inimitable Roshi Kapleau-fashion, "To Elsie, Porky, and Donald." (His Zen was clearly very Western and was from "inside" the culture, not an add-on.) He traveled to the Galapagos, that rough Eden, to see animals up close who had no ingrained fear of humans. He enjoyed spending time in rural Mexico, where he could walk down dirt lanes and see horses and cows wandering about on their own, going their own ways, and where he could go out, too, and stand by the wire fence and talk with the great black bull, Negrito, who lived in the field nearby.

He was such an unusual man for his generation. While he could be devastatingly logical and had a sharp mind, honed to a fine edge for literal detail, when speaking about myths and legends, especially those of the Buddha, he would say with the deepest kind of quiet respect, "Myth is truer than mere fact can say." He was a vivid storyteller who regaled us with tale after tale about his training days in Japan and his times with Nakagawa Roshi, Harada Roshi and Yasutani Roshi, about the military war trials, and about his own travels in Asia as well. The history of Zen in the twentieth century was in his blood, breath and bones.

One of his favorite stories from his own experience of Zen training involved the time he and an American philosophy professor were culled from the zendo one night at an early sesshin in Japan. Dutifully they appeared before the roshi, glad to have an official reason to get up off the mat and straighten their aching legs.

"What did Christ say when he hung on the cross?" asked the roshi. They looked at each other quizzically.

The professor said, " 'My God, my God,' wasn't that it? 'Why hast thou forsaken me? ' "

"Yes," Philip Kapleau concurred. "Yes. That's right. 'My God, my God, why hast thou forsaken me.' "

"No!" said the roshi.

This went on, back and forth several times, the two Westerners more and more sure that they had gotten it right, the roshi always disagreeing. At last the roshi burst out, the words surging up directly from his *hara* with stunning force, "What he said was, 'MY GOD, MY GOD, WHY HAST THOU FORSAKEN ME!' " When Roshi Kapleau would tell that story at night during sesshin, a gale of spirit would blow through the zendo, sweeping everything but pure yearning, aspiration and determination away. You had to be there.

In countless ways, from the vividly dramatic, to those that were simple, quiet and almost below-the-radar, he taught me and so many others how to place our feet on the path. He also taught me in particular, and with an equal ardor, where to put my commas. I knew how to make a sentence that had rhythm. He appreciated that. But he saw too that I knew little or nothing of punctuation. I broke a sentence mostly by breath. He loathed that and gave me hell for it! Which reminds me—one of the first times I met him, more than thirty years ago, he pointed out that in pulling up my car to speak to him I had parked too far from the curb. The implication was that if I stayed where I was I would make it difficult for others to pass. I re-parked and was more careful about such things after that. I saw that even the most seemingly inconsequential things I did had consequences.

He changed my life in both large—make that vast—and small ways. Given his many books, his teaching—both of the formal variety as in dokusan, teisho and sesshin, as well as through the informality of daily interactions and conduct—he affected untold lives. Though he is gone for now, his commitment to the endless fulfillment of Bodhisattva Vows guarantees that he will be back, and soon. Where, and in what form, old friend, shall we meet again?

13

On Zen and Failure

The essay, *Zen Failure* is based on a Dharma talk I originally gave at the Rochester Zen Center back in 1990. Later published in *The Sun* magazine it was also reprinted in *Progressions: Readings for Writers*. (Hilbert, W.W. Norton, 1998). I've left things in it pretty much as it was written, some thirty years ago. I still find it relevant and thematically aligned with the Way of the Bodhisattva, and so, with this book.

In an earlier chapter of *A Zen Life of Bodhisattvas*, we explored a koan in which Manjusri, Bodhisattva of Wisdom, failed both to get close to the Buddha and to bring a young woman out of samadhi. Wu-men's verse for that koan says that this failure was "wonderful indeed." A Buddhist legend also related earlier in this book, says that Avalokitesvara, Bodhisattva of Compassion, gained the great power and skill of 1,000 arms and 11 heads through *failure*. And in the section on the Buddha as *The Bodhisattva*, in the jataka of the naga king, the Buddha in a past life makes a mistake and fails, and then, by correcting course, comes to an even fuller commitment to his Great Vow. Through failure his commitment to the Path of the Bodhisattva is matured and deepened.

For many reasons this is simply the way of things and is only natural. Failure is a necessary part of the Bodhisattva Path because it is a necessary part of anyone's growing up, a necessary aspect in gaining any kind of skill—musical, artistic, athletic, and so on. No one starts off where they want or hope to be. We see what's possible, and then from there, it takes work to reach that lofty goal. And work means coming up short again and again. Which is how we improve. Zen Buddhist tradition says that to achieve *full* understanding and *unlimited* compassion (which, paradoxically, Zen also says is already ours, though we don't yet know it), will require even more than one lifetime's work. In fact, it is likely to be a many lifetime effort. When Roshi Kapleau passed someone on an initial koan, he would point to the edge of the sitting mat and say, "Congratulations. You have gotten onto the edge of the mat. Your journey all the way across the mat—a journey of lifetimes—now begins." So we should expect failures along the Way, each offering a new opportunity to improve and mature in understanding, in ability, in character. What was once good enough, in time is outgrown, and turns out to be, "not yet enough." The bodhisattva suffers from a divine discontent. Our failure is wonderful, indeed.

In any case, here's a written form of the talk, *Zen Failure*.

"Zen failure" can mean many things. It could mean the failure of Zen; it could mean that someone is a failure in Zen; a Zen-like failure, or the Zen of failure are also implied. It's a potentially vast field. In the short time we have we'll only be able to touch the very tip of the iceberg of Zen failure.

For many years practicing Zen I thought I was a failure. But as more years went by I began to realize that failure is the heart of Zen. In fact, failure is what Zen is about. Perhaps it's what life is about. Successes never seem to last. Death, after all, comes in the end to take all success away. If you want something abiding, something for the long run, look to failure. There's a profundity to it. I don't mean giving up. I don't mean turning around and walking away. I mean the failure that we really have to work hard for, the failure we put everything into. Bitter failure. There's a kind of principle involved here which says that real failure requires real effort and is its own reward.

There's a little poem by Yeats, which came to me as I was thinking about this subject. It's "The Four Ages of Man" from "Supernatural Songs." I'd like you to think about it in relation to failure as the essence of the spiritual life:

> He with body waged a fight
> But body won: it walks upright.
> Then he struggled with the heart;
> Innocence and peace depart.
> Then he struggled with the mind;
> His proud heart he left behind.
> Now his wars on God begin;
> At stroke of midnight, God shall win.

There it is, failure, the last defeat of all one's hopes, fears, stratagems and efforts. The thing we fear, the ultimate defeat, the final failure is something that keeps me practicing; this growing recognition of the reality of death.

At some point during the course of the winter and early spring of 1990, with Rose's mother's death and then, two months later, my own mother's passing, came the recognition that all our efforts will come to naught. Each of us will die. Everything we have gained, everything we have worked hard for, all of it will be taken from us. Everything will be lost. Thoughts, feelings, the singing of birds, the cool wind on your skin on a hot day; all of these things, the sunrise and the sunset, the people you love — all gone! And then you realize your children will be gone, the children that you worry about, that you hover over in your mind, day and night. Gone. They're going to die, no matter how hard you work protecting them in this life, no matter how well they do as they grow up. And then you realize that your grandchildren will die. And your great grandchildren will die. And this has been going on since the very beginning. And it will go on as long as there's Time. So underneath all our successes, perhaps, after even a lifetime of successes, we still have to come face to face with this insurmountable failure.

Yet, it's interesting that in the Yeats poem we catch some glimmer that failure may not be as bad as we think. Would it be so bad if God won? And, through that little doorway, that narrow path, narrow as a razor's edge, opened by that doubt, we come to Zen.

Let me take a more mundane path, though, first. We're all failures and that's why we're in Zen. Maybe spiritual life is failed worldly life. And here's a little something we can talk about later: Is lay life simply failed monastic life? Or is it something else? Something different. Whatever it is, it's something I think we'll all have to sort out in the years to come. In any case I'd like to start with the mundane recognition that failure is a two-edged sword. There's the failure that prevents you from living fully, the failure built of fears and expectations, patterns to which mind and body have been long habituated. There's the failure that prevents you from hearing the birds singing, the failure to use the amazing and intricate senses of body and mind with which we've all been so lavishly endowed. There's the failure to get something we want, perhaps that's the failure we know best. There is also the failure that tempts our will and tests our mettle, reveals our desires and values. And then, there's the failure that's open and pure, the failure, if you will, that Zen is all about. What could be more ridiculous, after all, than working so hard, sitting and sitting, sesshin after sesshin, letting go of hope upon hope, facing fear after fear, desire after desire, to find out you have to fail completely in the end. You have to die the Great Death, the death of ego attachment. You have to give up Everything. You worked so hard, and now you have to die. Ultimate failure. And yet that's where "success" in Zen can begin.

As I said, we're all failures. We start off complete and whole (I am thinking now of memories of early childhood; no lack there, no unfulfilled desires) but after a while, trained perhaps by the world we see around us, we discover that we want to be handsome or beautiful. We want to be always loved and respected. We want, too, to be independent and strong. Perhaps we'd like to be wise. And certainly eternal. But somehow none of those things ever quite work out. It's not as we planned or hoped. And the failure becomes so bitter that we have to

On Zen and Failure

do Something. Perhaps we hear about Zen. We begin practicing. And for many years it's like we're shooting at a target but we keep missing. Failure after failure. But one day we find the failures are related to what seems to be success. Still, after having gained this, then, what? How many of us can truly accept that Zen truly offers Nothing? That, too, is another little failure, perhaps, we may encounter on the Path.

Anyway, through a number of failures I came to Zen. Certainly the pain of those failures was bitter enough to drive me onto a completely different path, the path of actual practice, practice in which you put the books away and your knees hurt. And then, looking back over life and the things we've done since Rose and I have been here in Rochester, there's the wonderful, glorious failure of the Oxcart Bookshop, which, for anyone who was here for it, was something to be remembered. A great failure, indeed! It took much effort to engineer that one! It all fell apart and then, a great surprise! Something new emerged, even better that what had been.

After the closing of the Oxcart I had an idea for a book. It was a book that went deep into some very painful parts of my life. At one time I lost everything, including my ordinary mind, and lived in backwoods Pennsylvania in redneck, backwoods situations. There was an old quarry behind a hill, and I thought I could take a wish from my childhood, a wish that had never and could never come true, and combine it with some of the feelings I had had while walking through that quarry, and make something new, as well as heal some old areas within myself. Anyway, for three years I worked on this story of a boy and the power of his imagination. For three years, (and this was after I had already written what became a very successful children's book), my manuscript was turned down by my editor. Failure after failure. Time and again. A hundred rewrites on this one little story: turned down each time. Then suddenly, as I was about to bite the bullet on the story, I saw in one timeless instant, how the whole thing could work.

After three years of effort, three years of failure, in thirty seconds it was written. Voila! And the book became a success. That period of loss and pain from many years ago gave me the basis to create something new, something that worked well and pleased me greatly. How do you explain it? Is failure terrible? Can it be a good thing?

One day when I was young, my father looked into my room where I was sitting on my bed drawing and said, "Don't become an artist." I worried about that for a long time. Could be a real mistake. Could be a big failure. Could be loneliness. Could be worse. Anyway, I failed to follow his advice, and ended up in the arts after all.

I had a talk with him a couple of years ago as he was driving me to a performance I was giving north of New York City and I said to him, "You know, the people I respected most when I was young were not really successes." I knew there was someone he and I both respected very much: the painter Van Gogh. I said something like "Van Gogh never sold a single painting while he was alive and died in poverty and mental pain. And William Blake, who I revered, died in poverty too (but in great joy). And then there's Melville who, after writing perhaps the greatest American novel and one of the greatest books in the world, got only terrible reviews and lived the rest of his life in obscurity and, finally, despair. These people seemed to be failures. Then there are people who are successes. They earn a lot of money. Maybe they make weapons. Maybe it's just some innocuous product that pollutes the environment a bit. (I'm not putting money, or success down; these are extreme examples to make a point.) Anyway, they have money, take good vacations, wear nice clothes, and naturally we think of them as successes. But the legacy they leave doesn't last long, and if it does, it's often something we don't want around anyway. But Van Gogh, Blake, Melville: their works just get stronger and stronger. How do you explain this? What is a success, anyway? What is a failure?"

Let me tell you a little story: an old story from China called the

"Green Pillow Dream." It was turned into a Noh play later on in Japan and was changed a lot but the essence of the story goes like this: Once there was a person who was dissatisfied with his life. He was a farmer. So he set out on the road, to seek his fortune. He walked for a day and then got hungry. He came to an inn nestled in the foothills of the mountains. He went in and as he didn't have much money, ordered a bowl of rice and some tea. And he was very tired at that point. So he was going to lie down and rest until the meager meal was served. In this inn was an old man, and the old man said, "If you're going to lie down, why not use my pillow?"

Now, pillows in ancient China weren't soft, bulky things. They were ceramic. It'd be like putting your head on a plate. But it's shaped to your neck and your shoulders when you lay your head down on it. And this was a beautiful green, glazed pillow. Before he put his head down on the pillow, he had a brief conversation with the old man, who asked where he was going, and also mentioned that it must be nice to be young and healthy. The young man said though he was, indeed, young and healthy he wasn't happy. He just worked all day in the fields and had nothing to show for it. Anyway, the old man gave him the pillow, and the young man put his head down and fell asleep.

The next thing he knew he was walking through a tunnel. He comes out the other end into a road running through an open field. He sees mountains in the distance, waterfalls flowing like silver, birds and horses and running deer, and tigers, too, in those distant mountains. He starts walking down the road that runs through the field and he comes to a village. A beautiful girl comes running out of the biggest house and calls him by name. She's been waiting for him she says. They get married, and soon he's running the estate for his wealthy father-in-law. He and his wife have children. In time he becomes Governor. When barbarians invade, he's called to lead the armies and, just like that, achieves a great victory, driving the invaders before him like dust before the wind.

He's made Prime Minister. The land flourishes like never before. Great successes, follow one after another.

But some of the other ministers become jealous and set up a plot, producing forged letters that seem to show that he's been working with the barbarians to overthrow the empire. And so he's banished. He loses everything. Great success becomes terrible failure. He's banished along with his wife and his children to a little country estate, a kind of hovel, where guards watch them by day and night. He has no privacy; he has no peace. He has nothing. He would, he realizes, have been happier, as an unknown farmer than living like this.

Eight years go by, then, a rider arrives with a scroll from the Emperor. The Emperor has discovered the plot and asks for forgiveness. All this man's lands are restored. His sons now are old enough to help rule. They become great generals and ministers, and again the land flourishes under his care. In time becomes a very old man, and he's lying there dying. After all his successes the final failure comes at last. The emperor has sent the best doctor in the world, but it's hopeless. There's nothing to be done. Tears flow. The emperor, his sons, his daughters, his grandsons, his granddaughters, his sons-in-law and daughters-in-law and his old wife are all crying. He leaves this world. He finds himself walking in a tunnel. He walks through and opens his eyes. He's lying in the inn with his head on the pillow, and the rice and tea are just being put down on the table. Hardly a moment has passed.

In the *Gateless Barrier*, there is a koan in which Manjusri, Bodhisattva of Wisdom, tries to awaken a young woman out of meditation. He tries and tries to no avail. He fails. Then a beginner bodhisattva from 10,000 or so worlds below this one tries and is immediately successful. Part of the verse to the koan goes: "A god mask, a devil mask / The failure is wonderful indeed."

Thinking of reality itself, quantum theory suggests that each moment arises out of a field of endless potential and has, in turn, an endless range of possibility extending from it. But, all those endless lines of quantum possibility collapse into the one line we know as "reality." All those other possible lines, now unseen or unrealized in our world, are ... failures. Ordinary reality is itself the perfect expression of failure that is wonderful indeed!

Easy enough to say, but we all know failure personally, and is it "wonderful indeed"? Is there something precious about failure? There is a verse in Zen, which has always meant a great deal to me, which goes like this: "When your bow is broken and your last arrow spent / Then shoot, shoot with your whole heart."

We are bound, it seems, for failure – or is it success? A final word: I don't want people thinking they should go out and fail at something; that this will somehow be good. If you do that you'll only be successes, successful at failing. Failure comes as you try to succeed. You don't have to make a special effort. It happens quite naturally. So just forget all of this. In fact, don't fail to do it.

Teeny Tiny Tower #1
Photo art by Ariya Aladjem Wolf

14

Painting of A Rice Cake: Creative Imagination and the Way of the Bodhisattva

This essay/think-piece initially appeared in 2010 at the website "Sweet Cake Enso," where it was created to accompany a traveling exhibit of Zen art then touring American Zen centers. The original photo art, (three large full-color pigment prints) "Teeny Tiny Towers," was created by my daughter, Ariya Martin, (the artist Ariya Aladjem Wolf). Based in New Orleans (Bulbancha) she is co-founder of the non-profit One Bird; a founding member of the female photography collective Southerly Gold, a member of Serpentine Choir, and teaches photography in the fine arts department as an Assistant Professor at the University of New Orleans.

> If you say a painting is not real, then the material phenomenal world is not real. Unsurpassed enlightenment is a painting. The entire phenomenal universe and the empty sky are nothing but a painting. Since this is so, there is no remedy for satisfying hunger other than a painted rice cake. Without painted hunger you never become a true person.
>
> *Zen Master Dogen, "Painting of a Rice Cake,"*
> *(Trans., Gary Snyder, Mountains and Rivers Without End.)*

> When [the Dharma] ... is internalized it is most naturally taught in the form of folk stories: the jataka tales in classical Buddhism, the koans in Zen.
>
> *Robert Aitken Roshi*

Painted rice cakes, it's said, can't satisfy hunger. How could they? It would be like reading a menu and expecting that to nourish us – this is how one traditional Zen view puts it. To be satisfied, we're told, we have to sit down and eat. To satisfy our real existential hunger, we have to sit down and actually practice. We've got to eat a real meal, bite into, chew and swallow a real rice cake. But Dogen brilliantly states, "There is no remedy for satisfying our hunger other than a painted rice cake." (*Shobogenzo* – *Eye of the Treasury of the True Dharma*, "Gabyo" – "Painting of A Rice Cake.")

No remedy for satisfying our deep hunger other than a painted rice cake? A painting of a rice cake is going to do the job – is actually the only thing that can?

Hmmm. So, is it that without illusion, imagination, dreams we can't be whole, can't fulfill the potential of our realization of this very moment? Without stories of previous exertions, without temples, teachers, thangkas, painted and carved Buddhas, altars, Centers, Shakespeare, zendos, Beethoven, Blake, Gandhi, Dogen, Mary Oliver, Gary Snyder, Martin Luther King, Tarzan, Ryokan, Rembrandt, Rothko, Hakuin, Hamlet, Gandalf, Frodo, mothers, fathers – who would we be? How would we proceed?

Dogen goes on to say in the section titled "Gabyo" of his *Shobogenzo*, that the idea of ourselves as either unenlightened or enlightened is itself a painting built of the five skandhas. Likewise the rooted idea of self and other is such a painting. Buddhas themselves are paintings created with clay shrines, a blade of grass, limitless aspiration, the thirty-two marks, and countless kalpas of assiduous practice effort.

If this is so, then what kind of truth would we seek, what kind of truth could we actualize that is not a painting? How would we become whole, that is, be satisfied, without a painting of a rice cake?

For it is out of the imagination that we create our real lives. Athletes know this better than scholars. If you want to swim better, visualize yourself in the pool, the water flowing smoothly past, the chiming, churning sound of that flow, the kick of your legs, the perfect effortless stroke. What happens in the imagination affects us, even makes us who we are. As Yeats says, "In dreams begin responsibilities." Stories, paintings, art itself is a tool that our ancestors worldwide passed down to us, an impressive technology, if you will, to refine the inner life, to improve our dreaming. To paint a picture.

This goes against the grain of a certain contemporary view that Buddhism, especially Zen, is not about dreams and imaginings, but rather about "reality" and "truth." The salvation Buddhist practice offers is, in this view, freedom from all such old-timey "fluff." I have even encountered some Zen practitioners who hold that imagination is the furthest thing from Buddhism, and, indeed, useless to its practice.

But we could just as well assert the opposite – that Buddhism, Zen included, is a great engine of wish and dream. In fact, the Bodhisattva ideal, the core of Mahayana Buddhism of which Zen is one aspect, might be said to depend almost entirely upon the power of Imagination itself. To vow to save all beings one must not simply imagine, but one must imagine bravely, totally, immensely, and deeply. Why commit oneself to a small dream, tediously emptying a vast ocean by the teaspoonful, when a great dream can encompass everything, even Truth itself, and swallow up the entire universe in a single gulp?

Of course, "imagination," like "myth," can for us, today, summon quite opposing connotations. The popular meaning of myth, like imagination, is that it is something "false." But myth can also mean something so true it cannot be put into one final linguistic or imagistic form. It underlies all forms. It is a story truer than words can say.

As for imagination, it need not mean fantasy, reflection, daydreams, thoughts, insights, or the stream of internal vision and thought, where we are isolated, withdrawn, and separated from whatever is right before us: that teacup; this bug. That damned leaky faucet. It can just as authentically mean Imagination, in the sense of infinite creative potential, the realm we might enter in meditation (zazen) when body and mind fall away; emptiness that is neither static nor dull, but free (empty) of all limitation; that is, a realm of infinitely creative potential, the realm out of which we dream/create our own unique daily, never-to-be-repeated, moment-by-moment, breath-by-breath, thought form-by-thought form, lives. It is where the highest we can imagine is the same as what IS, the state one might experience in watching the night dances at Zuni Pueblo where plants, birds, thoughts, galaxies, and stars enter the plaza as living, dancing beings. "There is a dream dreaming us," is a Bushmen saying pointing to this realm. It is the Empty realm of Reality. Blake says, "The imagination is not a State: it is the Human existence itself." And what is that? It is simply, "To see a world in a grain of sand, / And a heaven in a wild flower, / Hold infinity in the palm of your hand, / And eternity in an hour." (W. Blake, "Auguries of Innocence")

So, what we most usually term "reality" is, as it turns out, simply another dream, an imagining and a somewhat limited one at that. In the end, reality and imagination, Mind and stories cannot be separated. Painted cakes do feed our hunger. Not only are they not two, they are not even one: "In other words, myth is reality and reality myth. Dogen did not believe ... in a dualism between reality and myth ... rather his purport was to clarify, purify, and reinforce myth—that is, Buddha-nature – in order to see and touch reality as it was." (Hee-Jin Kim, *Eihei Dogen: Mystical Realist*)

Again, to repeat Dogen himself:

> If you say the painting is not real, then the material phenomenal world is not real, the Dharma is not real. Unsurpassed enlightenment is a painting. The entire phenomenal universe and the empty sky are nothing but a painting. Since this is so, there is no remedy for

satisfying hunger other than a painted rice cake. Without painted hunger you never become a true person.

One of the central koans (literally "public record") in the venerable *Gateless Gate* (*Wu-men kuan*; *Mumonkan*) collection of koans and commentaries by the early thirteenth century Chinese Zen Master Wu-men (Mumon as he's known in Japan) is its second case, "Pai-chang's Fox." The case itself is essentially a folktale about karma and essential nature in which a head priest is reborn 500 lifetimes as a fox. Wu-men's pithy comment on the case ends, "If you have the eye to see through this you will appreciate how the former head of the monastery enjoyed his five hundred happy blessed lives as a fox."

Here Wu-men might be making a sly reference to jataka tales—stories of the Buddha's former births, often in animal form. In the jataka tradition, the Buddha himself lives (essentially) five hundred past lives, before stepping forward and making his final, total effort to embody the Way, thereby becoming Shakyamuni, the Buddha of our own historic period. Wu-men's reference touches an interesting and classic point—were any of those 500 previous lives any less "Buddha"? The Zen question here is—are any of our lives now?

The voice of a mythic, deeply imaginative Zen runs like quicksilver through the koans, turning back and forth on fundamental points of karma and essential nature. And behind that, lie pointers to the Buddha's past lives as brought to life through the Dharma folklore of the jatakas, little paintings, snapshots of moments on the Way, all part of the traditional context of Buddhist practice and aspiration. They show the Buddha painting his own picture of Buddha, an enso (Zen circle) portrait, with the brush and ink of countless kalpas of sustained and dedicated practice.

***

In Ariya Martin's "Teeny Towers" one surface meets another in a clambering balancing act of daily aspirations. Containers at a modest bathroom sink—familiar to our hands in weight and shape and barcoded—summon grand triumphs in small daily actions. Intimate, domestic spaces are the scene of our own placing, where we often contemplate our actions in more administered spaces. Here, the symbolic imagination has been invited into the measured placement of one thing atop another in the midst of precarious life.

Appendices

Zen Chants

Sixteen Bodhisattva Precepts

The Three Refuges
I take refuge in Buddha.
I take refuge in Dharma.
I take refuge in Sangha.

Three General Resolutions
I resolve not to create evil.
I resolve to practice all good Dharmas.
I resolve to save the many beings.

Ten Grave Precepts
I resolve not to kill but to cherish all life.
I resolve not to steal but to respect the things of others.
I resolve not to misuse sex but to be caring and responsible.
I resolve not to lie but to speak the truth.
I resolve not to give or take drugs that confuse the mind but to keep the mind clear.
I resolve not to speak of the misdeeds of others but to be understanding and sympathetic.
I resolve not to praise myself and downgrade others but to overcome my own shortcomings.
I resolve not to indulge in anger but to exercise restraint.
I resolve not to withhold spiritual or material aid but to give them freely where needed.
I resolve not to defame the Three Treasures but to cherish and uphold them.

Great Vows for All (The Four Vows)
The many beings are numberless,
I vow to free them all.
Greed hatred and ignorance rise endlessly,
I vow to abandon them all.
Dharma gates are countless,
I vow to wake to them all.
Buddha's Way is unattainable,
I vow to embody it all.

Zazen Wasan—**Zen Master Hakuin's Chant in Praise of Zazen**
From the beginning all beings are Buddha.
Like water and ice, without water no ice,
outside us no Buddhas.
How near the truth yet how far we seek,
like one in water crying "I thirst!"
Like a child of rich birth
wand'ring poor on this earth,
we endlessly circle the six worlds.
The cause of our sorrow is ego delusion.
From dark path to dark path
we've wandered in darkness—
how can we be free from the wheel of samsara?
The gateway to freedom is zazen samadhi—
beyond exaltation, beyond all our praises,
the pure Mahayana.
Observing the precepts,
repentance and giving,
the countless good deeds,
and the way of right living
all come from zazen.

Thus one true samadhi extinguishes evils;
it purifies karma, dissolving obstructions.
Then where are the dark paths that
lead us astray?
The pure lotus land is not far away.
Hearing this truth, heart humble and grateful,
to praise and embrace it,
to practice its wisdom,
brings unending blessings,
brings mountains of merit.
And if we turn inward
and prove our True-nature—
that True-self is no-self,
our own Self is no-self—
we go beyond ego and past clever words.
Then the gate to the oneness
of cause and effect
is thrown open.
Not two and not three,
straight ahead runs the Way.
Our form now being no-form,
in going and returning we never leave home.
Our thought now being no-thought,
our dancing and songs are the
voice of the Dharma.
How vast is the heaven
of boundless samadhi!
How bright and transparent
the moonlight of wisdom!
What is there outside us,
what is there we lack?

Nirvana is openly shown to our eyes.
This earth where we stand
is the pure lotus land,
and this very body the body of Buddha.

Prajna Paramita Hridaya (*Heart of Perfect Wisdom*)
The Bodhisattva of Compassion from the depths of prajna wisdom saw the emptiness of all five skandhas and sundered the bonds that create suff'ring.

Know then:
Form here is only emptiness, emptiness only form.
Form is no other than emptiness, emptiness no other than form.
Feeling, thought and choice consciousness itself
are the same as this.
Dharmas here are empty, all are the primal void.
None are born or die. Nor are they stained or pure,
nor do they wax or wane.
So in emptiness no form, no feeling, thought or choice,
nor is there consciousness. No eye, ear, nose, tongue, body, mind;
no color, sound, smell, taste, touch or what the mind takes hold of,
nor even act of sensing.
No ignorance or end of it, nor all that comes of ignorance:
no withering, no death, no end of them.
Nor is there pain or cause of pain or cease in pain or noble path
to lead from pain, not even wisdom to attain, attainment too is
emptiness.
So know that the Bodhisattva, holding to nothing whatever
but dwelling in prajna wisdom, is freed of delusive hindrance,
rid of the fear bred by it, and reaches clearest nirvana.
All buddhas of past and present, buddhas of future time

through faith in prajna wisdom come to full enlightenment.
Know then the great dharani, the radiant, peerless mantra,
the supreme, unfailing mantra, the Prajna Paramita,
whose words allay all pain. This is highest wisdom,
true beyond all doubt, know and proclaim its truth:

    Gate, gate
    paragate
    parasamgate
    bodhi, svaha!

Bibliography

Aitken, Robert. *The Gateless Barrier.* San Francisco, CA: North Point Press, 1991.

———. *The Mind of Clover: Essays in Zen Buddhist Ethics.* San Francisco, CA: North Point Press, 1984.

———. *Original Dwelling Place: Zen Buddhist Essays.* Washington D.C.: Counterpoint, 1996.

———. *The Practice of Perfection: The Paramitas from a Zen Buddhist Perspective.* New York, NY: Pantheon Books, 1994.

Arntzen, Sonja, trans. *Ikkyu and the Crazy Cloud Anthology: A Poet of Medieval Japan.* Tokyo: University of Tokyo Press, 1986.

Blyth, R.H., *Haiku: In Four Volumes.* Tokyo: Hokuseido Press, 1952 – 1974.

Bradbury, Ray. *The Martian Chronicles.* New York, NY: Doubleday, 1962.

Bradshaw, G.A., *Carnivore* Minds: *Who These Fearsome Animals Really Are.* New Haven, CN: Yale University Press, 2017.

Chatwin, Bruce, *The Songlines.* New York, NY: Penguin Group, 1988.

Cleary, Thomas, trans. *Book of Serenity.* Hudson, NY: Lindisfarne Press, 1990.

Cleary, Thomas & J.C., trans. *The Blue Cliff Record.* Boston, MA: Shambhala Publications, 1992.

Cook, Francis Dojun, trans. *The Record of Transmitting the Light: Zen Master Keizan's Denkoroku.* Boston, MA: Wisdom Publications, 2003.

Cowell, E.B., ed. *The Jataka or Stories of the Buddha's Former Births. Translated from the Pali. 3 volumes.* 1895. Reprint, London, GB: Pali Text Society, 1973. Distributed by Motilal Banarsidass, Delhi.

Dresden, Mark J., trans. *The Jatakastava, or Praise of the Buddha's Former Births,* vol. 45, part 5 of New Series. Philadelphia, PA: Transactions of the American Philosophical Society, 1955.

Erdman, David V., ed., *The Poetry and Prose of William Blake*. Garden City, New York: Doubleday & Company Inc., 1965.

Govinda, Lama Anagarika. *Foundations of Tibetan Mysticism*. New York, NY. Samuel Weiser, 1971.

Hearn, Lafcadio. *Kwaidan: Stories and Studies of Strange Things*. Rutland, VT: Charles Tuttle, 1971.

⎯⎯⎯. *The Buddhist Writings of Lafcadio Hearn*. Intro. by Kennth Rexroth. Santa Barbara: Ross-Erikson, Inc., 1977.

Kapleau, Philip. *The Three Pillars of Zen*. Revised and Expanded Edition. Garden City, NY: Doubleday, 1988.

Kato, Bruno, trans, with W.E. Soothill, Wilhelm Schiffer, Yoshiro Tamura. *The Three Fold Lotus Sutra*. New York, NY: Weatherhill, 1975.

Kim, Hee-Jin. *Eihei Dogen Mystical Realist*. Somerville, MA: Wisdom Publications, 2004.

Koroche, Peter, trans. *Once the Buddha Was a Monkey: Aryasura's Jatakamala*. Chicago, IL: The University of Chicago Press, 1989.

Martin, Rafe. *The Banyan Deer, A Parable of Courage and Compassion*. Illustrated by Richard Wehrman. Somerville, MA: Wisdom Publications, 2010.

⎯⎯⎯. *Before Buddha Was Buddha. Learning from the Jataka Tales*. Somerville, MA: Wisdom Publications, 2017.

⎯⎯⎯. *The Brave Little Parrot*. Illustrated by Demi. Somerville, MA: Wisdom Publications, 2023

⎯⎯⎯. *Endless Path, Awakening within the Buddhist Imagination: Jataka Tales, Zen Practice, and Daily Life*. Illustrated by Richard Wehrman. Berkeley, CA: North Atlantic Books, 2010.

⎯⎯⎯. *The Hungry Tigress: Buddhist Myths, Legends & Jataka Tales. Completely Revised & Expanded Edition*. Cambridge, MA: Yellow Moon Press, 1999.

_____. *A Zen Life of Buddha*. Manotick, ON. Canada: The Sumeru Press, 2022.

McDaniel, Richard Bryan. *Further Zen Conversations: on the scope, practice, and future of North American Zen*. Manotick, ON: Sumeru Press, 2023.

Melville, Herman. *Moby Dick*. New York, NY: The Modern Library, 1992.

Oregon, Stephan and Braunmiller, A.R. *The Complete Pelican Shakespeare*. New York, NY: The Penguin Group, 2002.

Powers, Richard. *The Overstory*. New York, NY: W.W. Norton, 2019.

Mitra, Rajendralala. *Nepalese Buddhist Literature (Sanskrit Buddhist Literature of Nepal)*. Calcutta, India: Asiatic Society of Bengal, 1882.

Reischauer, Edwin O. *Ennin's Travels in T'ang China*. New York, NY: The Ronald Press, 1955.

_____. *Ennin's Diary: A Record of a Pilgrimage to China in Search of the Law*. New York, NY. The Ronald Press, 1955.

Rhys Davids, T.W., trans. *Buddhist Birth Stories (Jataka Tales): The Commentorial Introduction Entitled Nidana-Katha, The Story of the Lineage*. London: George Routledge & Sons Ltd; New York; E.P. Dutton & Co., n.d.

Rotman, Andy, trans. *Divine Stories: Divyavadana Part 1*. Somerville, MA: Wisdom Publications, 2008.

Safina, Carl. *Beyond Words: What Animals Think and Feel*. New York, NY. Henry Holt and Company, 2015.

Sasaki, Ruth Fuller, Iriya Yoshitaka, Dana R. Fraser. *The Recorded Sayings of Layman P'ang: A Ninth-Century Zen Classic*. New York, NY: Weatherhill, 1971.

Shaw, Sarah, trans. *The Jatakas: Birth Stories of the Bodhisattva*. New York, NY: The Penguin Group, 2006.

Shibayama, Zenkei. *Zen Comments on the Mumonkan*. New York, NY: New American Library, 1974.

Snyder, Gary. *This Present Moment: New Poems*. Berkeley, CA: Counterpoint, 2015.

Tanahashi, Kazuaki, trans. *Treasury of the True Dharma Eye: Zen Master Dogen's Shobo Genzo*. Boston, MA: Shambhala, 2010.

Tolkein, J.R.R. *The Lord of the Rings*. (3 vols.) Boston, MA. Houghton Mifflin, 14th printing.

Van der Post, Laurens. *Heart of the Hunter. Customs and Myths of the African Bushmen*. New York, NY. William Morrow, 1980.

Waddell, Norman, trans. *Complete Poison Blossoms From A Thicket of Thorn: Hakuin Zenji*. Berkeley, CA: Counterpoint, 2017.

_____. *Wild Ivy: The Spiritual Autobiography of Zen Master Hakuin*. Boston, MA: Shamble Publications, 1999.

Waddell, Norman and Abe, Maso, trans./annotated. *The Heart of Dogen's Shobogenzo*. Albany, NY: State University of New York Press, 2002.

Watson, Burton, trans. *The Vimalakirti Sutra*. New York, NY: Columbia University Press. 1997.

Wu, John. *The Golden Age of Zen*. Taipei, Taiwan: United publishing Center, 1975.

Hakuun, Yasutani, trans. Eido Tai Shimano. *Eight Beliefs in Buddhism*. Jerusalem, Israel: Youval Tal Ltd, 1966.

www.ingramcontent.com/pod-product-compliance
Lightning Source LLC
Chambersburg PA
CBHW021917180426
43199CB00031B/135